To- Fannie Mae
From - Pat
christmas 2012

GREATER THAN THE MOUNTAINS WAS HE

See note P. 145 &146

Johannes (1692)-1767 m AnnaMarie
            (1835)
|
George 1722 m Elizabeth Crubb
|
Jacob (1749) m Isabella Weitzel
       1839
|
Peter (1790) m Mahala Evans
       1855
|
John + Jane Nickolson
|
Sarah + Albert Cragg
|
mgt. Jane + Frank Baker
           (1877-1964)

WILMA HICKS SIMPSON

GREATER THAN THE MOUNTAINS WAS HE

The True Story of Johann Jacob Shook of Haywood County, North Carolina

TATE PUBLISHING
AND ENTERPRISES, LLC

Greater Than the Mountains Was He
Copyright © 2013 by Wilma Hicks Simpson. All rights reserved.

No part of this publication may be reproduced, stored in a retrieval system or transmitted in any way by any means, electronic, mechanical, photocopy, recording or otherwise without the prior permission of the author except as provided by USA copyright law.

The opinions expressed by the author are not necessarily those of Tate Publishing, LLC.

Published by Tate Publishing & Enterprises, LLC
127 E. Trade Center Terrace | Mustang, Oklahoma 73064 USA
1.888.361.9473 | www.tatepublishing.com

Tate Publishing is committed to excellence in the publishing industry. The company reflects the philosophy established by the founders, based on Psalm 68:11,
"The Lord gave the word and great was the company of those who published it."

Book design copyright © 2013 by Tate Publishing, LLC. All rights reserved.
Cover design by Rtor Maghuyop
Interior design by Jake Muelle

Published in the United States of America

ISBN: 978-1-62295-460-5
Biography & Autobiography / Cultural Heritage
12.12.10

DEDICATED TO:

To all who are doing genealogy research for the surname *Shook* and related families and to the generations of researchers coming after us.

ACKNOWLEDGMENTS

I must acknowledge the many people who have helped me gather information on the family of my great-great-great grandfather, Jacob Shook of Haywood County, North Carolina.

Persis, Foy, Doralyn, Brenda, Jean, Alice, Janice, Bob, Julian, and Paul. My gratitude for your help these eleven years has no bounds. I wish to thank those who have done proofreading for me.

I certainly must express my appreciation to Dr. Doris Hammett for her insistence that this book is needed and for her encouragement all along the way. I could not have done this without any of you.

TABLE OF CONTENTS

Preface 11
In the Beginning. 13
Chapter 1   Palatine History 15
Chapter 2   Immigrating 21
Chapter 3   Settling in Pennsylvania 33
Chapter 4   Shook Families Migrate to
            North Carolina 49
Chapter 5   Early Life in Catawba County 59
Chapter 6   Jacob in the American
            Revolutionary War 67
Chapter 7   Jacob After the War 85
Chapter 8   Taking Up Residence on the
            Pigeon River 91
Chapter 9   Life on the Pigeon River 95
Chapter 10 A New Spirit and a New Home 101
Chapter 11 How the House Was Used in
            Jacob's Time 111
Chapter 12 Shook's Campground Meetings 119
Chapter 13 Sundown for Jacob and Isabella 127
Chapter 14 Children and Grandchildren of
            Jacob and Isabella 139
Chapter 15 Jacob's Descendants in the
            Civil War 153
Chapter 16 The House as Jacob Built it 167
Chapter 17 The House After Jacob 171
Bibliography 179

PREFACE

This nonfiction story is based upon documents left by the first three generations of the Johannes Schuck Shook family in America, with focus upon Jacob Shook of Haywood County, North Carolina. When I couldn't find any existing personal documents for a peculiar event, I used documented historical information that anyone in the same situation and time period would have experienced. The chapter on the actual immigration across the Atlantic Ocean in 1732 is a prime example of my use of documented history.

I am privileged and humbled to tell you this story about my Great-Great-Grant Grandfather's life; and about his ancestors, his family and his resolute and extraordinary work for God. I have gathered genealogy information used herein since I first learned I was his descendant. There is much information out there and so much of it is incorrect. I do not claim to have found it all, or even that I have a complete understanding of what I do have. I do strive to give sources for everything that I have included here. You can choose for yourself what is fact and what is yet to be proven.

Jacob Shook's story did not end when he passed away on September 1, 1839. He still lives within the legacy that he left for his family and for all who have come to know about his life to this day. He and his wife, Isabella Weitzel Shook, raised eleven children, and they in turn also raised large families. His descendants are scattered over this nation. Everywhere they went, as they migrated from North Carolina, we find them working to establish communities where there had been none. They immediately set about to build a church and a school. Jacob Shook's descendants were pillars in their communities, and they are still unto this day. Over the decades there have been so many ministers of the gospel that they are uncountable. We are also teachers, lawyers, doctors, nurses, farmers, shopkeepers, laborers, and homemakers. Regardless of occupations, his descendants reflect his influence and his love for God, for family, and for country. This book will have several contributors, including work written by Jacob's deceased 4th great grandson, Bob Jones. Bob was a descendant who loved and respected Jacob's story. Bob was proud to be a 'Shook Kid'. Each chapter contributed by a descendant other than myself shall be identified and credit given to each writer.

Wilma Hicks Simpson

IN THE BEGINNING

Johannes Schuck and his family lived in terror in Germany. Economical depression, religious, political persecution, and wars swept across the nation of Germany in the early 1700s. Our Schuck ancestors knew the fear of pain, persecution, harassment, starvation and death. These were happening all around them. Crops were destroyed in the fields, farm animals were killed or stolen. Homes and barns were burned. Men were beaten and often killed, women raped, children missing all across the land. Persecution was so heavy and so wide spread that whole families ran for their very lives, most often in the dark of night. Neighbors and acquaintances could not be trusted not to turn anyone in to the authorities with fabricated reports for the exchange of a small amount of money or some other perceived perk. Before we can follow the story of our ancestors in a new land we need to understand why they would leave their extended families and property to flee to America in 1732

PALATINE HISTORY

This article may be reproduced as long as it is not changed in any way, all identifying URLs and copyright information remain intact (including this permission), and a link is provided back to Olive Tree Genealogy http://olivetreegenealogy.com/).

by Loraine McGinnis Schulze
Copyright © 1996

The Palatinate or German PFALZ, was, in German history, the land of the Count Palatine, a title held by a leading secular prince of the Holy Roman Empire. Geographically, the Palatinate was divided between two small territorial clusters: the Rhenish, or Lower Palatinate, and the Upper Palatinate. The Rhenish Palatinate included lands on both sides of the Middle Rhine River between its Main and Neckar tributaries. Its capital until the 18th century was Heidelberg. The Upper Palatinate was located in northern Bavaria, on both sides of the Naab River as it flows south toward the Danube and extended eastward to the Bohemian Forest. The boundaries of the Palatinate varied with the political and dynastic fortunes of the Counts Palatine.

The Palatinate has a border beginning in the north, on the Moselle River about 35 miles southwest of Coblenz to Bingen and east to Mainz, down the Rhine River to Oppenheim, Guntersblum and Worms, then continuing eastward above the Nieckar River about 25 miles east of Heidelberg then looping back westerly below Heidelberg to Speyer, south down the Rhine River to Alsace, then north-westerly back up to its beginning on the Moselle River.

The first Count Palatine of the Rhine was Hermann I, who received the office in 945. Although not originally hereditary, the title was held mainly by his descendants until his line expired in 1155, and the Bavarian Wittelsbachs took over in 1180. In 1356, the Golden Bull (a papal bull: an official document, usually commands from the Pope and sealed with the official Papal seal called a Bulla) made the Count Palatine an Elector of the Holy Roman Empire. During the Reformation, the Palatinate accepted Protestantism and became the foremost Calvinist region in Germany.

After Martin Luther published his 95 Theses on the door of the castle church at Wittenberg on 31 October 1517, many of his followers came under considerable religious persecution for their beliefs. Perhaps for reasons of mutual comfort and support, they gathered in what is known as the Palatine. These folk came from many places, Germany, Holland, Switzerland and beyond, but all shared a common view on religion.

The protestant Elector Palatine Frederick V (1596–1632), called the "Winter King" of Bohemia, played a unique role in the struggle between Roman Catholic and Protestant Europe. His election in 1619 as King of Bohemia precipitated the Thirty Years War that lasted from 1619 until 1648. Frederick was driven from Bohemia and in 1623, deposed as Elector Palatine.

During the Thirty Years War, the Palatine country and other parts of Germany suffered from the horrors of fire and sword as well as from pillage and plunder by the French armies. This war was based upon both politics and religious hatreds, as the Roman Catholic armies sought to crush the religious freedom of a politically-divided Protestantism.

Many unpaid armies and bands of mercenaries, both of friends and foe, devoured the substance of the people and by 1633, even the catholic French supported the Elector Palatine for a time for political reasons.

During the War of the Grand Alliance (1689–97), the troops of the French monarch Louis XIV ravaged the Rhenish Palatinate, causing many Germans to emigrate. Many of the early German settlers of America (e.g. the Pennsylvania Dutch) were refugees from the Palatinate. During the French Revolutionary and Napoleonic Wars, the Palatinate's lands on the west bank of the Rhine were incorporated into France, while its eastern lands were divided largely between neighbouring Baden and Hesse.

Nearly the entire 17th century in central Europe was a period of turmoil as Louis XIV of France sought to increase his empire. The War of the Palatinate (as it was called in Germany), aka The War of The League of Augsburg, began in 1688 when Louis claimed the Palatinate. Every large city on the Rhine above Cologne was sacked. The War ended in 1697 with the Treaty of Ryswick. The Palatinate was badly battered but still outside French control. In 1702, the War of the Spanish Succession began in Europe and lasted until 1713, causing a great deal of instability for the Palatines. The Palatinate lay on the western edge of the Holy Roman Empire not far from France's eastern boundary. Louis wanted to push his eastern border to the Rhine, the heart of the Palatinate.

While the land of the Palatinate was good for its inhabitants, many of whom were farmers, vineyard operators etc., its location was unfortunately subject to invasion by the armies of Britain, France, and Germany. Mother Nature also played a role in what happened, for the winter of 1708 was particularly severe and many of the vineyards perished. So, as well as the devastating effects of war, the Palatines were subjected to the winter of 1708–09, the harshest in 100 years.

The scene was set for a mass migration. At the invitation of Queen Anne in the spring of 1709, about 7,000 harassed Palatines sailed down the Rhine to Rotterdam. From there, about 3,000 were dispatched to America, either directly or via England, under the auspices of William Penn. The remaining 4 000 were sent via England to Ireland to strengthen the Protestant interest.

Although the Palatines were scattered as agricultural settlers over much of Ireland, major accumulations were found in Counties Limerick and Tipperary. As the years progressed and dissatisfactions increased, many of these folk seized opportunities to join their compatriots in Pennsylvania, or to go to newly-opened settlements in Canada. There were many reasons for the desire of the Palatines to emigrate to the New World: oppressive taxation, religious bickering, hunger for more and better land, the advertising of the English colonies in America and the favorable attitude of the

British government toward settlement in the North American colonies. Many of the Palatines believed they were going to Pennsylvania, Carolina or one of the tropical islands.

Map of Palatine Germany

IMMIGRATING TO AMERICA

The family had lived for many generations in the rural countryside near Niederbronn, northern Alsace-Lorraine, near the border of France. We cannot know how long Johannes and his wife prayed about, discussed, and planned for this. We know the first thing they had to do was to dispose of all their property including any land they might have owned, their home and personal items other than the few things they would take with them.

The Johannes Schuck/Shook family who immigrated together were the following:

Johannes Schuck, born ca. 1692, and his wife Anna Maria, born ca. 1692, last name unknown, and their children Johann George born April 26, 1722; Maria Catharina, born May 17, 1724; Christina, born August 23, 1727; and Rosina Barbara, born December 19, 1730.

From records found by Persis Shook, as she researched the Shook family in Pennsylvania in May of 2001, we learn that Catherine Dorothea Shook, born 1719 in Mosbach, Germany, married Johann Jacob Jundt/Yount in 1741 in Pennsylvania. She died on March 19, 1780. Jacob Yount was born on August 8, 1714 in Niederbronn, North-Alsace, Germany. He died in 1760 in Whitehall Township, Northampton County, Pennsylvania. We have copies of Dorothea's will, handwritten in German and transcribed and printed.

A Jacob Shook descendant, Jack Ruple, commissioned Dr. Volker Jarren, a German researcher, in 2011 to search our Schuck family records in Germany. Dr. Jarren spent several weeks seeking anything at all that could be determined as being of our family. Not many of the very old records have survived the ravages of time and the wars fought there. Dr. Jarren was able to confirm that our family lived in Niederbronn-les-Bains in the Alsace-Lorainne area. He also found the four birth records for children listed above in the Niederbronn church records. This church was Evangelical Reformed denomination. Dr. Jarren did not find a record for Catharina Dorothea Schuck. He did not find any records for Johannes or anything of Anna Maria because we do not know what her last name was.

Greater Than the Mountains Was He 23

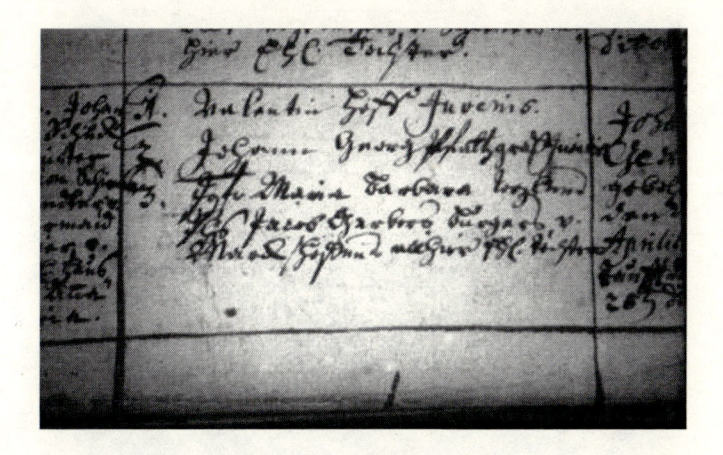

Birthdate of April 28, 1722 for Johann George Schuck in Niederbronn, Germany

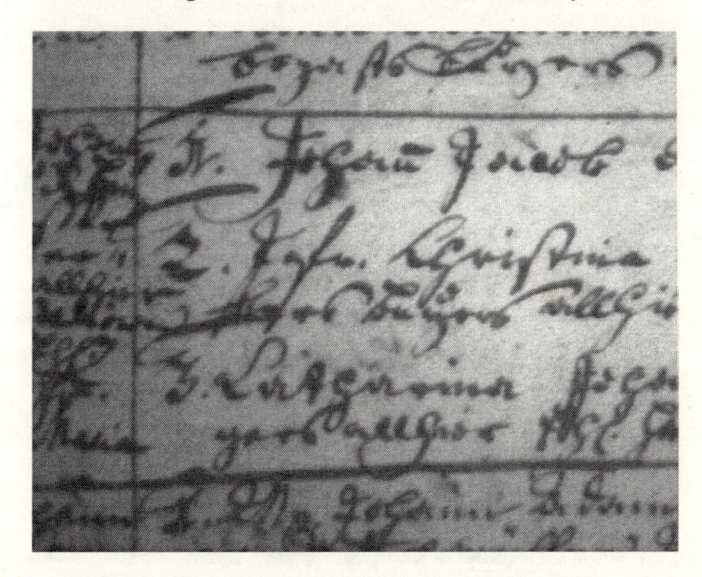

Birthdate of April 28, 1724 for Maria Catharina Schuck in Niederbronn, Germany

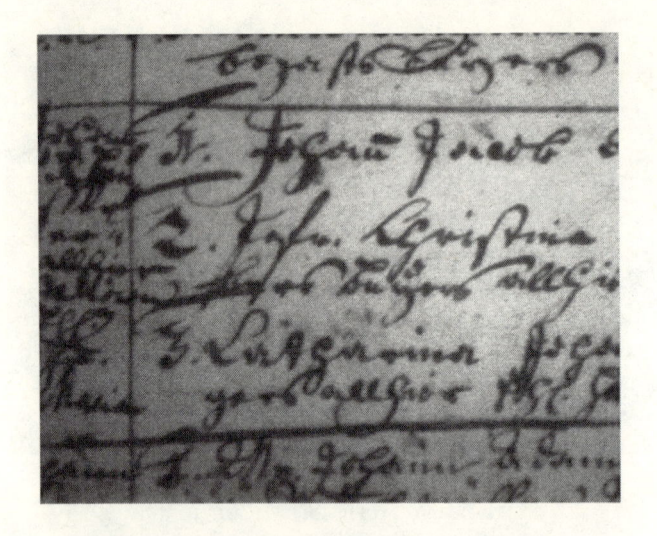

Birthdate of August 20, 1727 for Maria
Christina Schuck in Niederbronn, Germany

Birthdate of August 20, 1730 for Rosina
Barbara Schuck in Niederbronn, Germany

There is an *unproven theory* that we should talk about now. Some think that Johannes Schuck was married prior to marrying Anna Maria. Some think he had a first wife named Rosina Bernhard and that they lived in the area of Moebach, Germany. I have never seen anything in reference to this, but I understand that this information is out there. Catherina Dorothea may have been the daughter of this wife. The rest of this theory is that Dorothea may have immigrated to America the year before with the Jundt/Yount family. The Younts were neighbors with the Schucks in Germany, and she married Johann Jacob Jundt/Yount in America. I must stress that this is all speculation. This is one of the mysteries that we may never know as it lies buried two centuries in the past.

He did not find any records for Johannes or anything of Anna Maria because we do not know what her last name was. To summarize all the additional information that Dr. Volker Jarren provided after his extensive search, he gives this information: "Johannes was a master carpenter and at handicrafts in Niederbronn and from Evangelical-Reformed Denomination. In comparison to other people or godparents of his children he had not shared the rights of a citizen. He was an inhabitant only and therefore called here Schirmverwandter or Hintersasse. About his wife, it is only said that she was from the Evangelical denomination." Her maiden last name is unknown.

The family had lived for many generations in the rural countryside near Niederbronn, Alsace-Lorraine. This is the area that France and Germany fought over, and it has changed hands many times over the years. Some of these children may have been born there when the area belonged to France. We cannot know how long Johannes and Anna Maria prayed, discussed, and planned to immigrate. We know they had to dispose of all their property including their home and personal items. Families often walked away from their land after selling all they could to neighbors. They took with them only the most cherished items: the family Bible if they had one, a few tools, cooking utensils, food, warm clothing, bedding, and, when possible, a few desirable items with which to barter for supplies along the way.

The Johannes Schuck/Shook family who immigrated together are the following: Johannes Schuck, born ca. 1692; his wife Anna Marie, born ca. 1692, and their children were Hans George, Maria Catherina, Rosina Barbara, and Christina.

The Schuck family may have slipped away under cover of nighttime darkness and made their way to the Rhine river. The prevailing political atmosphere demanded that they make their plans in secret. Anything less may have triggered harsh treatments for the adults and sometimes the children. There were personal beatings, homes burned, livestock that disappeared on a regular basis for those trying to leave if their secrets reached the area governors. Families making their way to the Rhine would sometimes walk, carrying what they could on their backs. Those more fortunate had carts pulled by oxen or a small wagon pulled by a horse or mule. These were sold for whatever gain could be gotten from them once they reached the Rhine.

The Palatines boarded their small boats and headed down the Rhine for a seaport in Rotterdam and a new beginning. The river voyage took an average of four to six weeks. There were opportunists and scalpers all along the way who would hold the loaded boats for payment of differing sums before being allowed to proceed. Few would have been able to make it without help. An underground railroad was set up, and Protestant families along the Rhine gave sanctuary to the refugees as they made their way to the coast. Tent city refugee camps were set up for them in Rotterdam and for those who could find their way to England. Many families arrived at these camps without funds or property that could be used to raise funds. These families lived in these refugee camps for many months, sometimes years. All the family members, except the very young, would work at odd jobs until they could earn and save to pay for passage to America.

It is unknown how long the Schuck family had to wait in a refugee camp before finding passage to America. Johannes was a master carpenter in Niederbronn, and he would have had no problem at all finding work to fill the waiting period and supplement the family's coffers. Johannes was more fortunate than some because he had been able to sell most of his personal property to pay their fare.

Many immigrants sold themselves into bonded service to wealthy American entrepreneurs for years of labor in exchange for passage.

THE VOYAGE ACROSS THE ATLANTIC

The Johannes Schuck family found passage on the *Pink John and William,* meaning sloop, which was sailed by Captain Constable Tymperton from Rotterdam by way of Dover. There were seventy-one men, ninety-eight women, and children for a passenger total of 169. Sixty-one were Palatines. Eleven to twelve weeks was the expected duration of a crossing.

Passenger list on this ship's manifest listed Johannes Schuck and wife Anna Maria. Listed with them on the manifest were their son Hans (Johann George) and daughters Catherina Shooken (Maria Catherina?) and Maria Shooken (Rosina Barbara?) Was Catharina Christina, the oldest daughter, overlooked when the ship's manifest was drawn up? It is not for us to know in this life.

There are no documents to be found on the day-to-day life for the Schuck family as the voyage progressed across the ocean. There is, however, much written and documented general information that applied to these ships and their passengers of that time.

The accommodations were anything but comfortable. All passengers were quartered below decks, sometimes two decks below. Below decks consisted of one open room with posts and beams throughout that were supporting the deck above. These provided no privacy. Barrels of water, hardtack biscuits, salted fish and pork, oats for gruel, few miscellaneous ingredients for porridge and watery soup, and the least inexpensive rough food were on board for the passengers, these were stored in rooms that were inaccessible. The food was rationed out twice a day, and often even these things ran short, and rationing dropped to one meal a day. The crew had separate and better meals. There were livestock, pigs, and chickens on board, but they were meant mostly for the crew.

Families were encouraged to bring anticipated necessities as they could afford to purchase, such as food water, and medical supplies, including herbs. These supplies were to supplement the ship's stores. In reality, the ship's stores supplemented what the families could bring.

Space for each family was assigned below decks. This space was where the family lived the whole trip. It was measured out in just enough space for each adult to lie down, foot to shoulder to the neighbor. Children were given hammocks that swung above their parents lying underneath. Each family was given a pot for their bodily waste. It was to be emptied only once a day.

Body heat and odors quickly made the room's smell beyond description. Then all manner of illnesses broke out and quickly spread. Families were allowed onto the top deck to breathe fresh air for very limited periods of time, about an hour at best and on the best of days. As the voyage wore on, food supplies and fresh water dwindled and had to be even more strictly rationed. Mothers would be allowed an additional few spoonfuls of water a day for a fevered child. Dysentery was common. The very young and the elderly and those who had been exposed to illnesses prior to the beginning the voyage soon became ill, and some died without medical care. Toward the end of a voyage, food had been depleted except for the salted fish and pork. This salted fish and pork became all they had to eat. Water supplies would also be very low, and the salted food only increased everyone's thirst. This was double torment for the very young because they didn't understand. Many families lost more than one child and watched as they were buried at sea. The dead were wrapped in cloth if there were any rags available. Often the dead were tossed overboard naked. Clothing and shoes that could be used by another were always saved.

A family had to be in dire straits and with bleak futures in the old land before considering such a voyage, especially when they had infants and small children. The political and religious persecutions in Germany in the early 1700s created such a time when families would take a chance on the hope and prayers for a new life, a new beginning, in a new land.

Something went horribly wrong on this particular voyage. One speculation is that the captain, Constable Tymperton, went mad. Certainly, he lost control of the ship to the crew, who did not have the experience to finish the voyage. Finally, a few of the strongest male passengers took control of the ship and brought her into port. The vessel had been at sea seventeen weeks, six weeks longer than it should have been by the longest estimation and allowing for severe weather. There had been forty-four passenger deaths. Some deaths were by illnesses, but many were from starvation.

ARRIVAL IN AMERICA.

Benjamin Franklin's newspaper for that day records a mutiny, which took place on the ship, causing it to be much longer in transit than was usual at that time.

The mutiny was also reported in this newspaper:

> *The Pennsylvania Gazette*, Oct. 9–19, 1732
> No. 203 Custom House, Philadelphia
> Entered Inwards Sloop John & William
> Constable Tymperton, from Dover,
> Philadelphia, Oct. 19, 1732
>
> Sunday last arrived here Capt. Tymberton, in 17 weeks from Rotterdam, with 220 Palatines, 44 died in the Passage. About three weeks ago, the Passengers, dissatisfied with the length of the voyage, were so imprudent as to make a Mutiny, and being the stronger Party have ever since had the Government of the Vessel, giving Orders from among themselves to the Captain and Sailors, who were threatened with Death in case of Disobedience. Thus having Sight of Land, they carried the Vessel twice backward and forward between our Capes and Virginia, looking for a place to go ashore they knew not where. At length they compelled the Sailors to cast Anchor near Cape May, and five of them took the Boat by force and went ashore from whence they have been five Days coming up by Land to this place, where they found the Ship arrived. Those concerned in taking the Boat are committed to Prison. The fate of these men is unknown.

Upon arriving at the port of Philadelphia, all passengers were given the oath of allegiance to the British Empire and they were "qualified" immediately, meaning that they were either able to pay for their passage upon arrival, or they were met by someone already in America who was able to pay for them.

All immigrant families were required to qualify and take the oath of allegiance to England upon arriving on America's shores. This was done at the courthouse in Philadelphia. Qualified only meant that they were free of disease, the cost of their voyage and any debts were paid in full, and they had means of supporting themselves and would not become a ward of the colony.

> At the Courthouse of Philadelphia, October 17th, 1732. Sixty one Palatines, who with their families, making in all One hundred and sixty nine persons, were imported in the Pink John & William of Sunderland, Constable Tymberton, Master, from Rotterdam, but last from Dover, as by Clearance thence.

From the "Minutes of the Provincial Council," printed in Colonial Records, Vol. III, 466.

Our ancestors present at the courthouse in Philadelphia are listed as follows:

Johannes Schuck, Maria Shooken, Hans Shooken, Maria Shooken, Cathrina Shooken. Missing is Rosina Maria Shooken. She would have been a baby in her mother's arms and easy to miss.

SETTLING IN PENNSYLVANIA

The Shook family settled on an eighty-acre farm located in Williams Township in Northampton County, Pennsylvania. Williams Township is on the eastern edge of the state between the Schulkill and Delaware Rivers. It is located up against the peak where the Lehigh River runs into the Delaware River, about forty miles north of Philadelphia, on the outskirts of where Easton is located today. The first settlers arrived in Williams Township in 1725. Johannes Schuck was to live here the rest of his life. We have a copy of this land warrant, although it's not completely legible.

Even in Pennsylvania, German immigrants were treated as less desirable than British immigrants. The land available to them was way out on the outskirts of the English settlements. They were used as a barrier between the English settlement and the Indians. The land available for their purchase was not a choice land. The Schuck farm was rocky soil and was difficult to work. There were other German immigrants already living in their new community. It is almost certain that they were acquainted with some of these families and perhaps related in some way. Families in this community had everything in common. They worked with each other to build all types of necessary buildings. They built barns, sheds, and various types of storage buildings.

The first buildings they built were small cabins, probably with only one or two rooms. These were temporary shelters to be used while larger permanent homes were being built. Johannes had learned the post-and-beam method of building large homes and barns in the old homeland in Germany. Other German immigrants already living in the area also knew this method of building. It is little wonder that the Germans became known as clannish. They tended to stay together in the new world, establishing their own schools and churches, making their own lives there. They kept their old language for several generations. Johannes spoke his native tongue all his life, never learning the English language. Their lack of command of the language prevented them from serving in offices of the local government and forced them to rely on others to ensure whatever documents they might have need of were in order.

The Shook family was a member of the Old Williams Township Evangelical Lutheran Church, which was also known as the Congregation of the Delaware River belonging to the Lutheran religion. Many records of the Shook family marriages, communions, births, and sponsorships were to be found in the early records of this church. The Williams Church still exists today, along with the cemetery filled with old headstones inscribed in German.

p. 4	Johannes SCHNELL 14 Oct. 1740 19 Oct. 1740	parents: Johann Adam & Anna Margaretha	sponsors: Johannes Schuck & w. Anna Maria	
p. 4	Elisabeth DECKER Oct. 24, 1740 Nov. 26, 1740	Magnus & Christina	sponsors: Johannes Schuck & w. Anna Maria	
p. 6	Abraham LUN Sept. 17, 1743 Oct. 2, 1743	parents: Friederich & Anna	sponsors: Abraham LUN Anna Maria Schuck	
, p. 65	Marriage, Oct. 20, 1746, Johann Frantz MEHRBASS & Rosina Barbara SCHÜCK			
p. 65	Marriage, Aug. 8, 1748, Johann Georg SCHÜCK & Elisabeth GRUB			
p. 12	Johannes BRUCH b20 Mar. 1752	parents: Matthes & Anna Barbara	sponsors: Johannes SCHÜCK and wife _____	
p.70	Communicants, 6 Dec. 1750: Maria Catharina SCHUCKIN			
p. 71	Communicants, 17 May 1752: Anna Maria SCHUCKIN, Johannis's wife			
p. 72	Communicants, 22 Apr. 1753: AnnaMaria SCHUCKIN			
P. 73	Communicants, 1754: Anna Maria SCHUCKIN			

p. 142 List of members of the "Congregation on the Delaware River belonging to the Lutheran Religion" includes:...
John Adam SCHNELL, John SCHUCH, Magnus DECKER...Mathias BRUCH...Frederick LUNGER, Abraham LUNGER...Wilhelm VOL-BRECHT...Johan Frantz MEHRBOS...Andrew GRUB, Peter GRUB ...Michael KOCH..."George SHICK

additionally, from Pa. German Ch. Records, v. II, p. 50 (Williams Twp., Saucon, Northampton Co., Pa.):

Johannes Schück + wife Anna Maria, sponsors, with Philip Bossert, Jacob Scheimer, Michael Koch's wife Elisabeth ...

child:
Philip Jacob Dick
b. 4 Feb. 1750
bp. 11 July 1750

parents:
Johann Philip Dick
+ Sybilla Catharina

pg 1

Lutheran Church Record Page 1

p. 65, Lutheran Church Records of Williams Twp., Northampton Co., P
(Hoenstine Rental item #1432)

Marriage,
Aug. 8, 1748, Johann Georg SCHÜCK & Elisabeth GRUB

p. 9   Johann Jacob SCHÜCK   sponsors:
       7 April 1749   Johann Georg &   Andreas GRUB
       14 May 1749   Maria Elisabeth   Catharina KLEINHANS

p. 11 Michael SCHÜCK   parents: sponsors:
       10 Sept. 1751   Georg &   Michael KOCH
       29 Sept. 1751   Elisabeth   & Elisabeth

p. 16 Andreas SCHUK   parents: sponsors:
       21 May 1756   Georg &   Andreas RAUB
       27 June 1756   Elisabeth   Catharina GRUP

p. 13 Georg Fried. DICK   parents: sponsors:
       3 Aug. 1752   Friederich &   Georg SCHUCK
       16 Aug. 1752   Elisabeth   & Elisabetha

p. 14 Cath. Elis. GRUB   parents: sponsors:
       11 Sept. 1753   Andreas &   Georg SCHUCK
       30 Sept. 1753   Catharina   & wife Elisabeth
                                                    & Catharina GRUB

p. 67 Alms promised annually by Georg SCHUCK   2 s. 6 d.

p. 71 Communicants, 17 May 1752: Georg SCHUCK, wife Elisabeth

p. 73 Communicants, 1754 : Johann Georg SCHUCK, w. Maria Elisabeth

p.7   Joh. Georg   parents: sponsors:
       VOLLBRECHT
       28 Feb. 1746   William &   Joh. Georg SCHÜCK
       9 March 1746   Christina   & w. Rosina Barbara*

                           *This appears to be an error. Christina
                           (Schück) Vollbrecht/Fullbright's brother
                           Joh. Georg was not married yet, did not
                           marry a Rosina Barbara; Rosina Barbara
                           the sponsor probably is Christina's
                           unmarried sister.

p. 18 Eva Elis. JUNG   parents: sponsors:
       29 Jan. 1759   Melcher &   George SCHUK
       25 Feb. 1759   wife Catharina   & wife Elisabeth

p. 142 List of members of the "Congregation on the Delaware River
       belonging to the Lutheran Religion": Andrew & Peter GRUB
p. 143 (Same as above): Michael KOCH

p.146 List of alms promised:
       Christian Jacob SCHUK   ***
p.145 George SCHUK   2 Sh.

Lutheran Church Record Page 2

Nerbass, Franz Nerbass...Wilhelm Volprecht, w. Christina
...Georg Schuck, w. Elisabeth...

p. 73　Communicants, "Anno 1754, Dom: 10 P. Trin."
　　　...Frantz Nerbass, w. Rosina. Wilhelm Wolbrecht, w.
　　　Christina....Johann Georg Schück, w. Maria Elisabetha...

p. 142　List of Members of the "Congregation on the Delaware River
　　　belonging to the Lutheran Religion": Johan Frantz MEHRBOS

p. 8	Balthaser MEHRBASS 5 May 1747 17 May 1747	parents: Jacob & Anna Maria	sponsors: Philip Bodenwalder & w. Anna Maria
p. 9	Johann Phillip ODENWÄLDER 2 Feb. 1748 17 Apr. 1748	parents: Phillip & w. Anna Maria	sponsors: Jacob MEHRBASS Leonhardt KIEFER & w. Anna Maria
p. 9	Catharina LUN 28 Jan. 1749 5 Feb. 1749	Friederich & w. Anna	sponsors: Jacob NEHRBASS & w. Anna Maria
p.11	Johannes Franciscus NERBAS 15 Sept. 1750 28 Oct. 1750	Jacob & w. Anna Maria	sponsors: Johannes Franciscus NERBAS & w. Rosina Barbara
p.13	Maria Catharina NERBAS 23 Feb. 1753 8 April 1753	Jacob & w. Anna Maria	sponsors: Phillip Odenwälder & w. Anna Maria

　　* Hoenstine Rental item #1432
　　　Lutheran Church Records of Williams Twp., Northampton Co., Pa

p. 65　Marriage, Oct. 20, 1746,
　　　Johann Frantz Mehrbass ~ Rosina Barbara Schück

Lutheran Church Record Page 3

Information is expanded on all of Johannes and Anna Marie's children in the following pages.

Its purpose for being offered here is to expedite family background information that has bearing on Jacob's life. He was surrounded by his father's siblings, his aunts, and their family all his life.

Catharina Dorothea Shook—born 1719 in Mosbach, Germany—married Johann Jacob Jundt/Yount in 1741 in Pennsylvania and died 19 March 1780. Jacob Yount was born on 08 August 1714, in Niederbronn, north Alsace, Germany. He died in 1760 in Whitehall Township, Northampton County, Pennsylvania. In her will, written on 16 March 1780, and probated on 31 March 1780, Dorothea disinherited her eldest son, Peter, and a second son, Jacob, because they moved to North Carolina against her wishes. She left five pounds to each of their eldest children. The remainder of her estate she divided equally between her other four children: George, Daniel, Abraham, and Mary.

Maria Christina Shook, married Johann Wilhelm Volprecht/Fulbright ca. 1744, and died in March 1808 in Lincoln County, North Carolina. Johann Wilhelm was born in 1720 in Edelak, Schleswig-Holstein, Germany, the son of Hans Hiob Volbrecht and Maria Juditha Calenius. He died before 1808 in Lincoln County, North Carolina.

Some interesting notes taken from the publication *German-Speaking People West of the Catawba River* for Johann Wilhelm Vollbrecht / Fulbright. This is an example of just how badly some immigrants wanted to immigrate to America.

> When Wilhelm was seventeen years old, he was apprenticed to a great uncle in Basel, Switzerland to learn the weavers trade. From 1734 to 1740, he mastered his trade and the summer of 1740 traveled by Rhine river boat to Rotterdam, arriving practically broke.
>
> He was determined to migrate to the New World, so he indentured himself for five years and sailed on the ship "Robert & Alice" arriving in Philadelphia 3 December 1740. where he settled near Egypt, in Dutch Cove, Williams Township, in what is now Northampton County, PA. He is listed among those Baptized in 1746 in the church of the Morgan Hill Congregation and he and Christina were listed there as Communicants in 1753 and again in 1754. At that time the family is still spelling their name Vollbrecht. It seems they used this spelling until 1769 when they moved to North Carolina and settled on the north side of the Catawba River in what was first Rowan, then Burke, then Lincoln County before being changed to Catawba Co.

One of the Fulbright sons was Jacob, who married Elizabeth Wetzel/Weisel/Weitzel in Lincoln County. Jacob Fullbright was two years older than Jacob Shook. Jacob Fullbright served in the Revolutionary War, sometimes being stationed with Jacob Shook and his brother, Andrew Shook. After the Revolutionary War, he moved into Haywood County along with his cousins Jacob and Andrew Shook. Both Fulbright and Shook family researchers are searching for a link—possible sisters—between the two Weitzel women, Isabella and Elisabeth, but the Weitzel family has proven a difficult one to trace.

Rosina Barbara Shook married Johann Frantz Nehrbass on 20 October 1746 at the Old Williams Lutheran Church, where the family lived and attended church. They were listed as communicants of the church in 1752 and 1754. She was disinherited in her father's will.

Maria Catherina Shook married Henry Eigner. From old Johannes's will, it is known that Catherine and Henry Eigne Eigner were already in North Carolina by 1763. They had settled in what was then Rowan County. They were on the eastern bank of the Catawba River while the later folks settled across the river on the western bank. It is thought that she lived there the rest of her life.

Johann Georg George Shook, is the only son of Johannes and Anna Marie. George married Maria Elisabeth Grub, who was born in Germany on 8 August 1748. Johannes Jacob Shook was their firstborn. They were to go on and have six sons and one daughter.

It is every mother's heart's desire and dream for each of her children to grow up strong and to excel in all that life brings to them. Elisabeth was no different, and as she cuddled and nursed Jacob, a strong son, she dreamed of his future. Jacob grew to be a man in the community of Williams Township, Northampton County, Pennsylvania, and in Catawba County, North

Carolina. It was beside the Pigeon River, in his adult years and with his own family, that he would really find and fulfill the life that God had planned for him to live.

There are no records documenting his years as a youth. Yet we know he was educated well, having learned to read and write and having learned the math that carried him throughout his life. He learned the basics of the English language even though their native language, German, was the predominate language used in the community and, certainly, at home. He learned to build buildings and relationships. He learned the basics of blacksmithing and gun making, and he learned how to care for the farm animals that they were so depended upon. He was strong and healthy, and he could be relied upon by his extended family and neighbors in the community to help out with whatever needed doing. No doubt that he attended church services with his family on a regular basis. Still, the Lutheran religion left a hole in his heart that would not be filled for several years.

I found this article about naming children in Google Books, and I have inserted our Johann/Johannes for illustration:

> In the Palatinate it was customary to give children the names of saints, thus every child would be named after the patron saint of the family. It was common for a German family to name all of its sons John (the German word for John can be either Johann, or Johannes) with all but one of them having middle names. Only

if there was no middle name was the child actually called John. If the child was actually to be called John an "aes" was added making his name to be Johannes. Some traditions say that this way when the devil came for a child, he would become confused as to which John was which. Sometimes every girl would have the same common first name, for instance 'Maria', but not nearly as often as the males.

We see an interesting trend pertaining to birth records and naming of a child. Two dates are listed. Naming was not done until a baby was a few days old, usually a week, and the parents felt that this child was going to live through those first few days when child mortality was so high.

We see birth records listing for Johann Jacob Schuck, 7 April 1749 and 14 May 1749. (Johann meant he was to be called Jacob, and 14 May 1749 would be the date of his baptism.) Parents were Johann George and Maria Elizabeth Grub Schuck. Sponsors were Andreas Grub. We don't know whether he was an uncle or not. Life went on for the Shooks. There is no doubt they were happy here. They were enjoying all the freedom that their new home and new America had to offer.

This was what their dream had been back in the old country. The son and daughters grew to adulthood. Their life in the Delaware River church was such a joy compared to the restrained fear that they knew before. Here they made new friends with neighbors and renewed friendships with families known in Germany. The adult children found land of their own very close by or shared farming with Johannes. They were a close-knit yet extended family.

It is appointed in the life of every man and woman a time to die. Lives are lived out, and sundown years come to each of us. Johannes/John Schuck passed away in 1767. His wife, Anna Maria, passed away in 1772. She lived five years as his widow. Her date of death can be found on Johannes Inventory Sale and final distribution of his property.

Johannes/John Schuck/Shook left three documents for his descendants to find. We have a very poor copy of the land warrant for his farm in Pennsylvania. We have his last will and testament, and we have a copy of the list of his estate inventory.

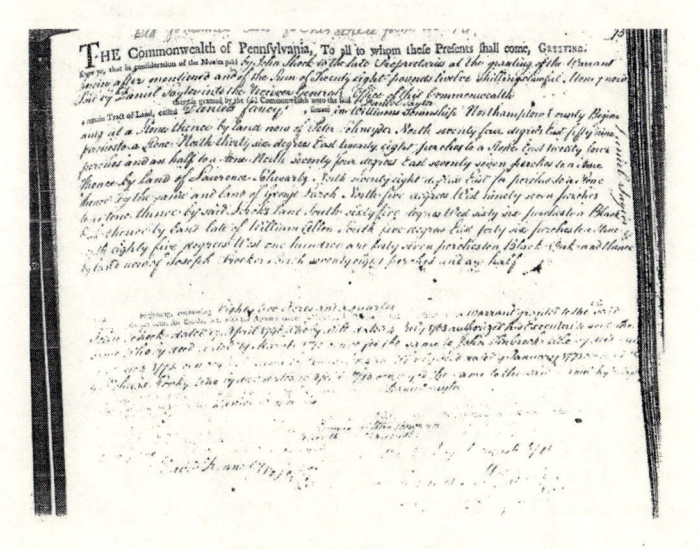

Johannes's land warrant in Pennsylvania

LAST WILL OF JOHANNES SCHUCK
[AND ESTATE INVENTORY SALE]

Copied exactly as written, including bad spelling and punctuation.

The fourth day of July in the Year of our Lord one thousand seven hundred and sixty-three, I John Schuck of Williams Township in the County of Northampton in the Province of Pennsylvania, being in good bodily Health, and of sound & well disposing mind & memory and being mindful of my mortality & desirous to settle my world affairs in the best manner I can , do make this my Last Will and Testament of and concerning all my temporal Estate in manner and form following (hereby Revoking all other Wills) that I do say First it is my Will that all my just Debts & funeral Expenses be duly paid. And I do give unto my Daughter Maria Catherina, wife of Henry Eigner of the Province of North Carolina Yeoman the sum of five Pounds lawful money of Pennsylvania. And I do give until my Daughter Rosina, the wife of Francis Nerbasse of Springfield Township in the County of Bucks Yeoman one shilling if the same shall be lawfully demanded which I will and ordain shall be in full of all her demands & Expectancy and of my Estate. And I do give unto my well beloved wife all and singular my Messaneges Lands Tenements and _____ whatsoever or wheresoever with Appurtenance To hold to her my said Wife Anna Maria and her Assigns for and during the Term of her natural Life without Impeachment of Waste. And I do will and devise that the Premisses upon the Decease of my said Wife shall be sold by my Executors hereinafter named and for that End I do hereby give full Power and Authority unto my said Executors & the Survivor of them & the Executors of the Survivor as soon as conveniently may be after the Decease of my said Wife to grant bargain and sell the same Premisses until any Person or Persons whatsoever his her or their Heirs and Assign for Ever for the best price and Consideration that can reasonably be gotten for the same. And for and concerning the Proceeds arising by such sale is aforesaid I do give and bequeath the same unto and amongst my Children namely George, Dorothea the Widow of Jacob Yount deceased, Christina the Wife of William Fulbright of the Township of Williamston aforesaid and the said Maria Catherina Part & Share alike and to their Several heirs Executors Administrators of Assigns. Moreover I do give until her my said Wife Anna Maria the use and occupation of all the rest and residue of my Goods and Chattels and personal Estate for and during all the Term of her natural Life and from and immediately after her Decease I would have what is left thereof to be equally divided amongst my said Children namely the before named George, Dorothea, Christina, and Maria Catherine. My meaning is not to lay my Wife under the Restraints of to make her or her Executors or Admen. responsible or accountable for anything that shall hereby come to my said Wife's Possession For I will not put her under the control of any of my Children. And I do hereby nominate and appoint my trusty Friends Christopher Bittenbender and Jacob Best both of Williams Township aforesaid Yeoman to be the Executors of my Last Will and Testament in Witness whereof I the said Johan Schuck have hereunto set my Hand and Seal the Day and Year first above written

his
John HS Schuck (Seal)
Mark

Signed, sealed & published & declared by the above named John Schuck the Testator for and as his Last Will & Testament in the Presence of us who in his Presence & at his Request have hereunto set our Hands as Witnesses to the same.

Andrew Schouby. Andrew Brockoch. J. Okely.

Northampton County on the twenty ninth day of December in the Year 1767 Before me Lewis Gordon personally appeared John Okely and Andrew Brochoch two of the Witnesses to the foregoing Last Will and Testament of John Schuck deceased and on their Solemn. Affirmation according to the Law do declare and say that th Will and Testament and that at the doing thereof he was of sound mind memory and understanding to the best of their knowledge and belief. And further that Andrew Schouby together with these Affirmants did sign his name as Witness thereto at the request and in the presence of the said Testator and in the Presence of one another. [Note: signed] Lewis Gordon.

Anna Maria, Johannes's wife, died on January, 23 1772, and the final distribution of Johannes estate was made on May 8, 1773.

We have a copy of the original estate inventory sale. It can be found in the courthouse of Williams Township, Northampton County, Pennsylvania. It is handwritten on a huge sheet of paper, and it is in very, very poor condition. A good copy cannot be obtained from it. Over the years, the folds in the paper have torn and were mended with Scotch tape. The tape has done more damage than the passage of years.

There is one expense listed as "cash paid for writing three releases from the Children." These were notarized by power of attorney given by the three children then living in North Carolina. Some sources say that George Shook returned to Pennsylvania to collect monies from his father's estate.

Four children each received 45-12-11 English currency when the final settlement was made. That would be about $76.00 today in 2011 exchange rate.

Grand total of his estate was 232-29-11 in English currency. With today's exchange rate of $1.65 to an English pound, his estate would have been around $386.

SHOOK FAMILIES MIGRATE TO NORTH CAROLINA

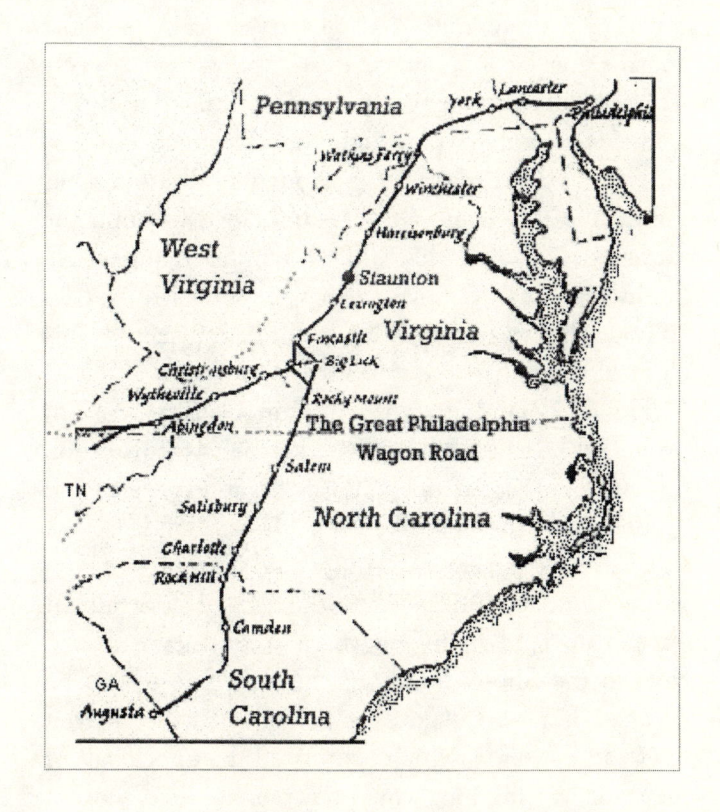

The Great Pennsylvania Wagon Road

The extended Shook family was growing. All the five children had married and now had families of their own.

All of them lived either on the farm with Johannes and Anna Maria or had found land to purchase and rent in the vicinity near their parents. Theirs was a happy family. We can picture in our minds the Sunday dinners and celebrations that they must have shared. Children added to the noise and bustle of their gatherings. By mid-1750, there must have been a dozen or more cousins for Jacob to play, work, and grow up with. Think about him being eleven years old, tall and reed thin. He would have thought he was much older as he tried to learn everything about life all around his family. No doubt he had already helped to build the numerous buildings that all farm families required. No doubt his aunt's families all had buildings to put up and building was a family affair. Life was sweet for this close-knit family.

However, land in Northampton County was not prime land. It was hilly and rocky, making cultivation difficult and crop yields lower than expected and needed. Still, the area filled quickly, and land became expensive. A fifty-acre farm would have cost seven pounds and ten shillings. As the federal government opened up land in the southern states, news filtered back to the Shook family of the rich, fine soil to be purchased in North Carolina. In the Granville District of North Carolina, which comprised the upper half of the state, five shillings would buy one hundred acres of prime land. This news was a very attractive deal for the Shook extended families to think upon.

We have found no documentation of the many conversations and hours of prayer they must have had in making the decision to leave part of their family in Pennsylvania and migrate to North Carolina. We do not know the exact year when they migrated. We do know that the Fulbright family went first. We have no personal documents to tell us what the trip was like for them. However, there is much historical general information of what all pioneers experienced as they traveled the Great Wagon Road to their new home in North Carolina.

Only a few trails cut through the vast forest, which covered the continent between the northernmost colonies and Georgia, the southern tip. The settlers, as they moved inland, usually followed the paths over which the Indians had hunted and traded. The Indians in turn had followed the pre-historical traces of animals. Few paths crossed the Appalachians, which formed a barrier between the Atlantic plateau and the unknown interior. In his 1755 map of the British Colonies, Lewis Evans labeled the Appalachians "Endless Mountains." And they must have seemed so to the daring few who pierced the heart of the wooded unknown. But through this unknown, even then, there was a road.

It grew from a foot path no wider than three or four feet, just room enough for a man or a horse and rider to pass in single file. Tree limbs brushed and grabbed at the traveler's clothing and skin. Then it was cleared and made wide enough for two-wheel carts pulled by oxen. All but the most elderly and the very young walked along the side of their carts and small wagons.

We can imagine boys, dirty from grim imbedded into clothing and skin. It may have been days or weeks since any of them had the opportunity to bathe in a creek or a river. Even then, bathing depended on the weather. The hasty rub that Mother gave to faces and hands before the evening meal could not have been much of a bath. The boys' duties were to drive an assortment of livestock, pigs, and milk cows and to lead the pack animals. Jacob would have helped his mother to see after his five younger brothers, and perhaps his baby sister, Sabillia, whom he adored.

We are not sure how old Jacob would have been when his father, George, and this extended family migrated to North Carolina. Jacob could have been a teenager. I can see him rested each morning from sleeping on the ground rolled in a blanket. In the morning, he would have jumped up full of energy and ready to chase a rabbit or throw a stone at a bird that was skittering through the trees. His energy would be gone long before sundown. If he was younger, we can hear him asking, "Are we there yet?" or "How much farther is it?" Children haven't changed that much. If Jacob was in his late teenage years, he probably did much work as a man. He would have put away his childhood pastime activities early.

Cart wheels wore out and broke frequently, as did wagon wheels. Rivers were difficult to cross with such vehicles. Many times, every item of their belongings got soaked, and much might have been lost in the rivers. Traveling was exceedingly slow. Under the best of conditions, the journey would take months.

By 1765, the Great Pennsylvania Wagon Road was cleared wide enough for horse-drawn wagons, and by

1775, the road stretched seven hundred miles. Inns, blacksmiths, and establishments selling services and goods were to be found along the way. This is not to say the journey was made easy for anyone, just less difficult.

I have summarized this description of Conestoga wagons to be found in Google Books. Oral history indicates that the Shooks may have had a Conestoga wagon. This, of course, is unproven. Other wagons used were ordinary farm wagons fitted with canvas covers.

THE CONESTOGA WAGONS

The Conestoga Wagons originated in Pennsylvania around 1750. They were popular for migration southward through the Great Wagon Road. These were the most desired of vehicles in colonial times if a family could afford one.

The Conestoga wagon was cleverly built. Its floor curved in such a way as to prevent the contents from tipping and shifting. The average Conestoga wagon was 18 feet long, 11 feet high, and 4 feet in width. It could carry several times more pounds of cargo than farm wagons. The cracks in the body of the wagon were filled with tar to protect them from leaking while crossing rivers. Also for protection against bad weather, a tough canvas cover was stretched across the wagon. The frame and suspension were made of wood, while the wheels were often iron-rimmed for greater durability. Water barrels built on the side of the wagon held water, and toolboxes held tools needed for repairs on the wagon. There was a feed box attached to back of the wagon that was used to contain feed for the horses. The term "Conestoga wagon" refers specifically to this specific type of vehicle.

However long it took, whatever hardships they met, we can visualize the family group resting at the end of each day around a campfire as they have their evening meal. Perhaps the older boys and men had been able to hunt and had been able to kill a young deer or a few rabbits as they traveled that day. Any fresh meat, fresh fish, wild vegetables and herbs that might have been gathered throughout the day would be greatly welcomed additions to the diminishing food stock. The adults would talk over the day's happenings and plan for the next day. They knew that there were small settlements along the way. These were thought of as landmarks along the trip and perhaps they would be reaching one of these the coming day. There they might be able to purchase something urgently needed such as a tool to replace a broken one. The women and mothers might be able to replace articles of clothing or shoes that were worn beyond repair. Children were exhausted after a day of travel and were put to bed to sleep after their meal. Perhaps the older children listened to the increasing night sounds and identified which animal had made that sound. Perhaps they watched the stars come out, and played games identifying each cluster. Later, there might have been singing, and certainly scriptures were read as they had their daily devotional and time of prayer. Eventually all would find their bedrolls and go to sleep, feeling thankful for being another day closer to their destination. The actual details of their days are not for us to know at this time. We do know they must have arrived at their destination worn down and physically exhausted.

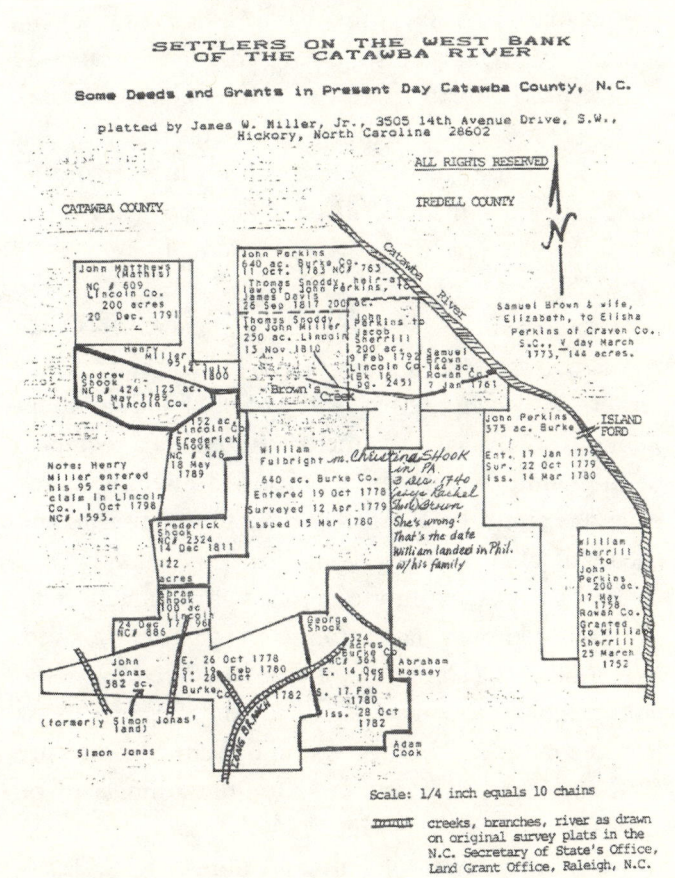

Settlers' map on the west bank of the
Catawba River

The source of this map is unknown. This old plat, mapped out by James W. Miller Jr., is interesting in that Lyles Creek is not shown on it. We do note that William Fulbright, who had married Christina Shook in Pennsylvania, registered 640 acres in 1778. This does not mean that 1778 was the year he arrived in Catawba County with his family. Oral tradition indicates he migrated to North Carolina before George Shook brought his extended family. We see on this plat that George and Elizabeth's sons established farmland all bordering their uncle William Fulbright's land. They are all here except Jacob. Speculation reigns here. Why not? Where was he?

The area on the west side of the Catawba already contained several other settlers. Some of these settlers may have been known by the Shook family in Pennsylvania. Certainly, there were enough members of the family and neighbors present to help George's extended family build small shelters for themselves and their animals.

It was a busy time for everyone with so much to do. We do not know what season or the year they arrived. Was it in spring so there would be a rush to clear some land and plant food for themselves and the stock? Was it in the fall, with the rush to build shelters and secure food for themselves and feed for the animals to be sufficient through the winter? We can only speculate. Maybe the Fulbright family and other friends knew that George was bringing more of their extended family and about when they would arrive. Perhaps temporary shelters and some cleared land were already done and waiting on them. Timber for these building had to be cut and brought to the chosen sites no matter the season. Everyone in a family had chores to do, even all the children, except the very young. Yes, we can spend hours thinking about how hard that first year in North Carolina was. Still it was not any harder than getting settled in Pennsylvania. Certainly, it was a far better life than what the older members would remember from their German homes.

There was another situation that added to the family's daily concerns. Roving bands of young Cherokee Indians were harassing the white settlers in Catawba County. These were young men who were not satisfied with the treaties in existence between the Cherokee and the white settlers. Nor would they listen to the council of their elders.

The Cherokee had been badly used by both the English and the French. Treaties were made and immediately broken. There was much resentment over the loss of their hunting lands. They were not proclaiming all-out war at that time, but they did burn crops, steal cattle and horses, and even burn homes occasionally. The settlers posted lookouts day and night to sound alarms if these young Cherokee bands were sighted.

Yet they thrived. German people are known to be very hardworking people. Their work ethic and persistence enabled them to settle in, put up buildings, clean land, and plant crops at an amazing pace. They established a Lutheran church and a school.

There was other trouble looming over the land like a morning fog. The colonial government was in agreement with England. There was much resentment on both sides. These were the days leading up to the Revolutionary War. Publications, such as they were, that reached the settlements along Lyles Creek told of grim things that were discussed every time neighbors gathered. There would be no rest now in the new lands. And Jacob would soon be caught up in it, along with his brother Andrew, and his Yount and Fulbright cousins.

EARLY LIFE IN CATAWBA COUNTY

As settlers moved into a new area, they found vacant land they wanted, and they settled on it without the benefit of immediately recording the land as theirs. Often, it was many years before land records were recorded. Some tradition says this was in 1765, and that they came to Carolina as a group however, the only evidence of this early arrival is the land granted to William Fulbright (Wilhelm Vollbrect) dated 1763 on Lyle's Creek in today's Catawba County, North Carolina. Jacob Fulbright, William's son, stated in his pension application many years later that it was actually 1769 when William brought the family to North Carolina.

Whenever they came is not for us to haggle over today. The fact that they were there on Lyle's Creek before the Revolution is not in dispute, and the story of Jacob Shook, the pioneer, must start with an understanding of that place and time. In London, it was called LORD Granville's Trans-Catawba; but to the Schucks, it was *Cataber* County.

Imagine if you will, a wild country, roadless and pristine. Look across the seemingly endless hills that are covered with trees. Look across and down into the many little valleys that are crowded with open prairies and cane thickets to see the beauty of the country. Here and there in this vastness, you might imagine on a cold winter's day a plume of smoke rising from some pioneer chimney. This chimney, upon closer inspection, would be of the "stick and mud" variety, attached to a log cabin hewn by the owner from trees that once stood nearby. The cabin might have one or two rooms with a lean-to attached. These could be extra tall to accommodate a sleeping loft for the children. A sleeping loft would have been built out over the lower room. It would be like a shelf. If a family had been there a few years, their home would have grown into something larger. A cabin would have two or three small windows covered with cloth or oiled paper. Out back, you would see a number of crude outbuildings serving as a stable for the farm animals, a corncrib, smokehouse, and blacksmith shed. On a plantation of 250 acres, about sixty acres might be cleared of trees and planted in some crop such as oats, wheat, and corn. Closer to the house would be the orchards and a garden of vegetables.

Threading through the wilderness, connecting these rare outposts, you might imagine a network of paths not much more than footpaths. These pathways from time to time might see the hooves of the occasional horse or oxen. Along these pathways one could find, if he imagined a trip along down Lyle's Creek, a household much like the last ones could be seen after walking about two hours. On Lyle's Creek in 1760, that distance was called a German mile. And on Lyle's Creek, that was exactly what it was, for the Dutch (Americanized version of Deutsch) had settled there in numbers after their long trek down the Great Pennsylvania Wagon Road.

The original land grants on Lyle's creek record the owners. Johan Baum in 1750 was the first recorded. Simon Yonoss (Jonas) and Hinrich Shrink, Phillip Hahn, Conrad Mull, Conrad Boobey, and Johann Hagins appeared soon after. Then in 1753, the German United Brethren, or Moravians, purchased a huge tract of land in LORD Granville's district, location undefined. They set out to determine the land they would select and brought a small team of surveyors across the Catawba to "look for the land." They hired Johann Baum as guide. Being duly impressed with the area between the South Fork of the Catawba and the Catawba proper, they decided the that area, which included Lyle's Creek, would be an ideal spot for their projected colony.

John Carteret, Earl Granville, set aside this huge parcel, as well as several others, for the Moravians and ceased to sell land there late in 1753.

For ten years, the land lay under this reserve. In 1755, the Moravians decided to place their colony at a less remote area, which is today Forsyth County, North Carolina. However, the restriction still remained on the Catawba lands until 1763. In that year, the land was released, and it seems that many German settlers had been living on the land in question without deed for up to ten years.

In 1763, many of them came to the land office in Rowan County at Salisbury, a two-day walk away from home, and registered their claims. The names from Lyle's Creek include Henry Pope, George Schmidt (Smith), Jacob Wissenaut, Adam Aker (Eckard),

Adam Bolch, Thomas Cowan, Peter Grunt, Michael Hart, Johan Haun, Andrew Killian, Isaac Lowrance, Peter Stutz, Christian Treffelstadt, Conrad, Joseph and William Whittenburg, and William Fulbright. (So there is our Jacob's aunt Christina's husband, Wihelm Vollbrect, in 1763.) Then in late 1763, John Carteret, Earl Granville, died, and his heirs in England closed the sale of his lands. It was 1778, fifteen years later, before the office would open again, and many, many Germans had come to live on the unclaimed lands by then. In December 1778, a total of 8,900 acres were registered in Salisbury on Lyle's Creek alone. Among these names, we find Christopher Beekman (Jacob's captain in the Cross Creek campaign); Adam Bolick, George, Peter, and William Deal; and George Eslinger, Peter Grant, Frederick Gross, Devault Hunsucker, Johann Isonhower, Frederick Shull, Andrew Fulbright, and our Johann George Shuke (Shook).

It was to be after 1770 before the first real congregation of German-speaking settlers began to form west of the Catawba. In those years, they were served by itinerate circuit riding preachers who would come from time to time to their meeting house built on the South Fork of the Catawba. This first church, Der Saut Fark in German, was the predecessor of "Old" St. Paul's Lutheran Church in Lincoln County, which still exists today. On the rolls of that church's early membership, as reported in 1775 by its first permanent minister Johann Arends (or Ahrend, Arent, Arnt, and Arndt as it is variously spelled in English records), we can find the Lyle's Creek surnames of Bolich, Hahn,

Hauk, Killian, Klien, Siegman, Wiegnburger, Miller, and Schuk (Shook).

Church was the only real authority in the area, for although the distant courthouse at Salisbury was technically the seat of civil power, its reach was weak on the west side of the Catawba, especially in the tight-knit German communities. The elders mediated disputes and organized community efforts such as barn raisings and cooperative harvests.

In the case of wills and other official court documents, documents that were often not accepted in German, the ministers often made translations for filing with the clerk in Salisbury. The evidence of the linguistics of the Shucks is lacking in this early period, but it does appear that Jacob learned to speak English well, despite evidence that German remained his primary language. History would tell us that George probably never spoke English at all. Jacob most likely had a very limited English vocabulary in Pennsylvania, but as he lived in "Cataber" Country, he probably became more or less fluent in that language, at least in a bare bones sort of way from necessity. Surely, after months of service with the militia on the frontier during the Revolution, he became more comfortable communicating with his English-speaking fellows, but I am sure English always remained his second language throughout most of his life.

Jacob most likely got his first encounter with the Cherokee Indian people early on as the families settled into their new homes. It is well documented in Cherokee history that they were under treaty with the

English government, and governors would not make war against white settlers. However, there were bands of roving young Indian braves who disagreed with these treaties and watched the white settlers night and day. Minor skirmishes, harassments, and thievery were perpetrated throughout the history of colonial America between white settlers and some portions of all various Indian people.

Today, there are approximately one hundred Shook names listed in the telephone directories of Catawba County. There is a winding county road named Shook Road, weaving in and around Lyle's Creek. The people living here are descendants of George's other sons who would be Jacob's nephews.

We refer to George and Elizabeth's time as being that of the second generation in America. No last will by either of them has ever been found to my knowledge. There is evidence by the many and frequent land transactions in his later years that he disbursed his property himself before he died. October 4, 1799, is the date of George's final deed, which they both signed in North Carolina.

George was born ca. 1724 near Niederbronn-les-Bains in the Northern Alsace-Lorraine near the German-France border. He married Elizabeth Grub in August 1748 in Old Williams Church, Northampton, Pennsylvania. He died after October 1799 in Lincoln County, North Carolina.

Elizabeth Grub Shook was born 17 March 1733 near Kusel/Cusel, Rheinland-Pfalz, Germany. She died after October 1799 in Lincoln County, North Carolina. We have no dates of their deaths, so we do not know exactly how old each were.

JACOB IN THE AMERICAN REVOLUTIONARY WAR

There was uneasiness all across the colonies. There were several contributing factors creating this. England and France had been in a continued state of war with each other over control of the new lands. Each solicited the Indian Tribes to their sides. There was a long history of Indian harassments against the white settlers. Often these were instigated either by the French or the English representatives in their efforts to gain control for their own governments. The Indian tribes were promised that their land would be returned to them if the white settlers were removed. So all these tribes were fighting for the return of their old way of life. The English government under King George III was well aware that they were losing control of the colonies. The new colonists felt the sting of increasingly higher taxes imposed on them by the English. The patriots were forming their own militia groups to protect their own homes and properties. The English military was alarmed at the number and strength of the ever-increasing patriot militia forces. The whole country was a cauldron of unrest and apprehension. Bits of news filtered through the settlements. Printed materials were rare and treasured when they would arrive in a neighborhood. They were read and passed on so that all the settlements were informed. Often these would be many weeks old and still being passed around. Increasing the uncertainty among the settlers.

In early 1775, news had come to the settlers about the British engagements with patriots at Lexington and Concord in Massachusetts. In May, a meeting took place in Charlotte, North Carolina, in which those assembled declared their independence from England in the Mecklenburg Declaration. Then in the summer of 1775, the royal government was pressed back to Wilmington by aroused patriots, and the royal governor called for all loyal citizens of the king to arm themselves. As pressure increased, royal governor Martin was forced to flee Wilmington and govern from a ship off the coast. Still, he hoped to rally support for the king by calling to arms the Loyalists, or Tories, of North Carolina. The center of Tory activity was in the area settled by the Scotch Highlanders at the Cross Creek settlement near today's Fayetteville, North Carolina. As rumors of this concentration of forces at Cross Creek spread, the new patriot government, sitting in Hillsboro, called for the formation of a North Carolina regiment to suppress the Tories.

WAR COMES TO WESTERN NORTH CAROLINA

In late 1775, Griffith Rutherford was appointed by the patriot government to recruit ten companies of militia from Rowan County to participate in this action. The call went out up the Yadkin and Catawba Valleys, and soon hundreds of men had come to Salisbury to answer the call. Twenty-six-year-old Jacob and his nineteen-year-old brother, Andrew Shook, were among the recruits. After a bit of drilling and marching to and fro about Salisbury, General Rutherford decided his men were as ready as they could be under the circumstances, and the ragtag little army marched off toward Fayetteville, eighty miles away, as the crow flies. This was in February 1776. (In his pension application, Jacob stated that this was in March 1775.) It's likely that old memories weren't that precise so many years later in 1834 when he applied for a pension based on his service.

This campaign resulted in the defeat of the Scottish Tories at Moore's Creek Bridge on February 27, 1776, north of Wilmington. Jacob and Andrew, with Rutherford, didn't make it to Moore's Creek in time for the battle, so they spent the month of March at Cross Creek, mopping up resistance and ensuring the submission of those of the Scottish rank-and-file who were captured at Moore's Creek and then returned to Cross Creek on parole. The Shooks were discharged, and they returned home to Lyle's Creek at the end of March.

Then on July 1, 1776, the Cherokee, who had maintained an uneasy peace with the settlers at the foot of the Blue Ridge since the end of the first Cherokee War in 1762, came screaming out of the mountains with tomahawks and scalping knives. The Cherokee nation had been coerced by British agents to attack the settlers all along the frontier from Virginia to Georgia. On the upper Catawba, just a few dozen miles from the homes of the Shooks on Lyles Creek, the Indians struck. General Rutherford wrote the new rebel government in Hillsboro the following letter concerning that attack on July 14, 1776. (The spelling and punctuation are Rutherford's.)

> Honorable Gentlemen,
> I am under the necessity of sending you by express, the Alarming Condition this country is in, the Indians is making great progress in Destroying and Murdering in the frontiers of this county. I am informed 37 was killed last Wednesday & Thursday on the Catawba River. I am also informed that Col. McDowell with 10 men and 126 women and children is Besieged, in some kind of a fort, with Indians all round them, no help to them before yesterday and they were surrounded Wednesday. I expect the next account to here that they are all destroyed. ... Pray Gentlemen, Consider our distress, send us plenty of Powder & I Hope under God we of Salisbury District is able to stand them, but, if you will allow us to go to the Nation, I expect you will order Hillsbourgh District to join Salisbury. Three of our Captains is killed and one wounded. This day I set out with what men I can Raise for the relief of the Distress. Your Humble Servant, Griffith Rutherford.

General Rutherford received the help he requested; the government at Hillsboro called out all the western militia, so Andrew and Jacob Shook, home only four months from the Cross Creek affair, now found themselves again in the service, this time marching west up the Catawba toward Davidson's Fort, now Old Fort, North Carolina. Here were gathered about 2,300 men. A wild mixture of militia, the North Carolina regiments and rangers from all over the state were all eager to once and for all put an end to the Cherokee threat. While the majority of these men were set to the work of acquiring supplies to feed the expedition, six hundred men were chosen to go into the mountains and feel out the Indian positions.

This brave band of soldiers, with Jacob and Andrew among them we believe, marched up the rugged path through the Swannanoa Gap in early August 1776 and then down the valley of the Swannanoa River to the French Broad. Crossing that river at the war ford three miles south of today's city of Asheville, near the Biltmore House, they camped for two weeks, waiting for the remainder of their forces and supplies to arrive. The creek they camped on got its name from this time; it is today called Hominy Creek, recalling that the only food the expedition had for those two weeks was hominy, or pickled corn.

With the arrival of supplies and additional troops, Rutherford marched on up Hominy Creek in mid-August and began to fight small engagements with the Cherokee. He passed across the high ground that divides Hominy Creek from the waters of the Pigeon River and crossed that river at the "Forks," moving downriver into a flat valley of open fields and huge virgin trees. Early settlers would later call the area "the

Gardens." Here Rutherford again waited for a time as he sent scouts deeper into Cherokee country.

The area where some of Rutherford's troops waited in on this stop would later become Clyde, North Carolina, and we can imagine Jacob and Andrew as they took in its wonders. They probably hunted the nearby hills of the Newfound Mountain range and fished the crystal waters of the Pigeon River and determined that when all this was over they would return to this spot. And they did, ten years later, to live and raise families.

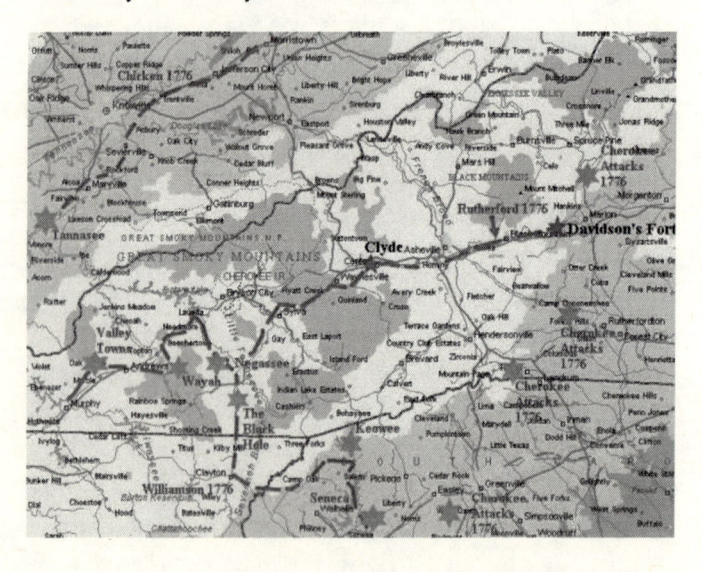

Revolutionary war route map through Clyde

JACOB IN THE INDIAN WARS

Ready to march finally, Rutherford broke camp and began to feel his way steadily forward. Several scouting parties would range ahead, guided by friendly

Indians. They might surprise a few enfeebled and old inhabitants as they broke from the woods upon a village, but in almost all cases, the warning of their coming had preceded them, and the inhabitants had taken to the hills. These scouts would summarily kill any inhabitants; no quarter was given for sex or age as indeed none had been given by the Indian attacks on the Catawba River settlement.

It was no wonder that surprise was impossible; the army moved at a snail's pace. Nineteen hundred and seventy foot soldiers, eight hundred light horsemen acting as scouts and guards, and fourteen hundred pack horses marched forward on the narrow path. Hours were spent clearing brush on the pathway so that a horse could pass.

Here on the only track through the forest, no thought had been put into their location by those who used it; if a man could step upon the earth, it was all that was needed, for on foot was the Cherokee's only mode of transport. The column, thus constrained, stretched along for miles. One foot soldier was employed as driver over every four horses and one pack master over each ten drivers. The column carried with them all the food and ammunition they would need for forty days.

Having bypassed the war parties, he was told they were lying in wait for him at Soco Gap. Rutherford had free reign over the towns along the Tuckasegee and Oconaluftee Rivers. The Cherokee women and children disappeared into the wilderness as the patriot forces approached, so the deserted towns were quick to go to the torch and to smoke and ruin. More than that, the crops in the fields were set ablaze, assuring a difficult survival in the coming winter months. The Cherokee forces opposing Rutherford now attempted to draw him west toward the Nantahala Gorge, and after leaving a sizable contingent on the Cowee Mountains to threaten the Cherokee middle kingdom's capital at Naquasse (Franklin, North Carolina) he moved after them. A sharp engagement was finally fought in which the Cherokee were driven away; this engagement is almost mythical in its lack of documentation. It appears to have been fought in the mile-high heights around Wayah Bald, one of the greatest mountains in the Nantahala Range, now on the Appalachian Trail.

Jacob and Andrew Shook now marched with Rutherford through the Nantahala Gorge and then down the Valley River, burning deserted towns and adjacent fields of maize ready for harvest as they went. Finally they reached the Hiawassee River at today's Murphy, North Carolina, where they stopped. Rutherford was supposed to go on if possible and meet the Tennessee troops on the Hiawassee River in today's Tennessee. His men, mostly militia, had done enough, they said, and winter was rapidly approaching in the rugged mountains. Short of food and ammunition, and having received no word from the Tennesseans, Rutherford decided that he must turn around. Before he could depart, Williamson and his troops arrived at the junction of the Valley and Hiawassee River (Murphy), and General Williamson concurred with the decision, so in late September, Rutherford began movement back along his own track, toward home, while Williamson turned south and moved through northern Georgia on his way to South Carolina.

The weary patriots marched out of the mountains and back to Davidson's Fort around the first part of October 1776. On his march home, Rutherford ordered that the route be marked and blazed so that future travelers could find their way. This trail has sense been known as the Rutherford Trace. Although General Williamson's troops had lost many more, Rutherford had only lost three of his North Carolina men. This was an incredible accomplishment, to say the least, considering they had routed the Cherokee. As the frontiersmen returned down the Swannanoa Gap across the crest of the Blue Ridge toward home, they believed they had broken the power of the Cherokee forever.

We can easily imagine that when Andrew and Jacob returned to their home on Lyle's Creek, they felt their duty to the Revolution had been served. They had started with the threats from both east and west and had marched to dispose both, placing themselves in harm's way. Now they probably hoped that the world would just leave them alone.

History tells us that the fragile society of the Cherokee middle kingdom was indeed broken, never to fully recover. Disease, starvation, and frozen death stalked the civilian population. Reduced to hiding in the most remote corners of the mountains in makeshift hovels and eating off the land, the Cherokee nation's leadership prayed for peace. Its military might was still extant, however, and refused the pleas of the elders. Broken into small bands, the Cherokee still put up many raids and attacks on those unfortunate enough to be caught unprepared. Before 1776 was out, Rutherford sent another troop, commanded by Captain Moore, who later settled on Hominy Creek, on a winter expedition to the Little Tennessee to Stecoah to destroy an area he hadn't reached in his attack.

By the summer of 1777, faced with horrible destruction leveled against their Cherokee kingdoms, with the withdrawal of British support due to their misfortunes in other areas, the Cherokee sought peace. Not all agreed, and many young hotheads left their home villages to pursue the war in uncontrolled bands.

At Due West, South Carolina, on May 20, 1777, and again at Long Island of the Holston in today's Tennessee on June 20, 1777, treaties of peace were signed, which gave away much of the Cherokee lands. To South Carolina went most of the Piedmont region, with assurances that the whites would leave the refugees of the lower kingdom alone in their new abodes in Northern Georgia. To Virginia went all Cherokee claims in Kentucky, and to North Carolina all of today's Tennessee west of the Tennessee River, north of the French Broad and east of the Pigeon River. The middle kingdom, whose ceded land was the valley of the French Broad and Pigeon Rivers in western North Carolina, claimed to have not been properly represented at that signing so this part of the cession later came into dispute.

In 1777 and 1778, things were a bit quieter, but small patrols were sent into the Cherokee nation, and often, companies of rangers were sent into the wilderness in pursuit of the occasional renegade raiding party. In the summer of 1779, there were renewed raids by both the militia and the Cherokee into each other's territory.

The war came in earnest to the Catawba settlement in late 1780 with the Battle at Ramsours Mill, followed by the American victory at King's Mountain. Although these events occurred only a few dozen miles from Jacob's home, we don't know the part he might have played in these events. All indications are that both he and Andrew stayed home during this period.

The situation on the frontier in the spring of 1781 was the result of a master plan conceived by the British commander Cornwallis. After his defeat at Cowpens in South Carolina backcountry the past January, which had been such a thorn in his side in the campaigns of 1780, Cornwallis determined that the patriots should have their attention diverted by attacks from his remaining Indian allies.

So during the winter, British agents were at work again in Cherokee lands, inciting the young warriors and passing out guns and ammunition. The settlers heard rumors of this, but it was obvious that the shortage of manpower due to the many actions of warfare in the local area would prevent any offensive moves into Indian country, so a defensive tactic was taken. When the somewhat desperate Indian attacks began in the early months of 1781, in support of the British effort, forts were garrisoned as never before, and large numbers of civilians moved under their protective guns. These forts were located to block the various pathways to and from the mountains, and regular armed patrols connected them across the foothills.

To provide the manpower for this system, a draft was put upon each county on the frontier. Those chosen by the local captain of militia were expected to turn out for the call. To be drafted, you must be a juror in good standing, have taken no parole, and be fit for service. Jacob fit these qualifications, so on May 10, 1781, he joined the command of Captain Smith at Davidson's Fort (today's Old Fort, North Carolina) on the upper Catawba as ordered. This was his third tour of duty.

It can't be known what Jacob's duties were at Davidson's Fort. As a private, he might have participated in patrols that took him once again to the Pigeon River at the site of future Clyde. Jacob must have often talked to others around the dusty stockade who made the regular patrols.

That summer, another campaign was launched from today's Tennessee that penetrated up the French Broad River. This campaign met the North Carolina patrols near modern Asheville. By this time, the continuing resistance, though substantial, was obviously the work of renegade bands, many of these led by Tory refugees. Now the militia spent their time with "lightning" raids into the mountains, with hopes to capture or kill the Tory leaders and their Indian allies.

Jacob returned home at the end of his enlistment in August 1781with papers of discharge in hand properly signed by a Captain Smith. Jacob had no way to know that just a few days after he returned home, on August 19, the veteran Continental Army commanded by George

Washington with his 6,500-man army slipped quietly out of their trenches in New York and headed south to surprise Cornwallis. Cornwallis had taken the British southern army to Yorktown in Virginia. Here General Washington met eleven thousand French soldiers with a large French fleet, which had surprised the British fleet off Cape Charles and sent it sailing back to New York. Cornwallis was trapped and outnumbered.

The British troops marched out of Yorktown October 19, 1781, to a ceremony of surrender. They were marching between ranks of blue-coated and buckskinned ranks of Americans and white-uniformed soldiers of the French. As they marched and stacked their arms, the British bands played the song "The World Turned Upside Down."

There would be other engagements as the war wound down, but British resolve had evaporated, as well as British support from the home islands. The British signed the Treaty of Paris in 1783 as part of a treaty intended to end the worldwide conflict that had grown between France and Great Britain.

With this treaty, the British agreed to evacuate the remaining areas of the thirteen colonies before year's end, and all the territories held east of the Mississippi River, with the exception of Florida, would be transferred to the realm of the fledgling United States. The Revolutionary War was over, and a new nation, under God, was born.

Most descendants now believe that this photo is of Johann Jacob Shook

Jacob Shook Revolutionary War Pension Application

State of North Carolina) JS
Haywood County)

On this 3rd day of October 1833 personally appeared in open Court before the honorable the judge of the Superior Court of law and Equity for said County of Haywood, being a court of record now sitting.

Jacob Shook, a resident of said County & state aged eighty four years who, being first duly sworn according to law, doth on his oath make the following declaration in order to obtain the benefit of the Act of Congress passed the 7th June 1832.

That he resided in what is now Lincoln County, North Carolina when he entered the service of the United States under the following named officers and served as herein stated (to wit) that in the month of March in the year 1775 as he now thinks he entered the service of the United States as volunteer in the company commanded by Captain William Bateman in the regiment commanded by Col. Christopher Bateman in the Brigade commanded by Genl Rutherford and marched to what was then called Bass Creek now Fayetteville, North Carolina against the _____ Tories. Which tour lasted one month or more, the precise time not now recollected. As a part of the Tories being taken and the balance dispersed before he reached that place, he remained at that place but a short time.

That on the 9th of August 1776 he served a tour as a drafted militia man against the Cherokee Indians in Captain Rudolph Conrad's Company in regiment commanded by Col. Christopher Bateman in the _____ commanded by Genl Rutherford and served two months.

On the 10th of May 1781 he was drafted for a three month tour against said indians and marched to Davidson's Station at the head of the Catawba River in what is now Burke County, North Carolina under Captain Daniel Smith, which time he served and was discharged by said captain on the 10th day of August in that year, which discharge is herewith transmitted. He received no discharge for the two first tours.

He was born in the county of Northampton in the State of Pennsylvania on the 19th of April in the year 1749 and is now eighty-four years of age. He has lived in the County of Burke, North Carolina since the revolutionary war and now lives in the County of Haywood in said state.

He has no record of his age. Was not attached to any continental regiment nor was he acquainted with any regular officer and has not any proof of his service, either documentary or the testimony of any person whose testimony he can procure that he knows of except that herewith transmitted.

Question 1st   Where were you born?
Answer In Northampton County in the State of Pennsylvania.

2nd Ques.   Have you any record of your age?
Answer I have none.

Jacob Shook's pension application, page 1

Jacob Shook Revolutionary War Pension Application *Page 2*

Quest 3rd   Where were you living when called into the service? Where have you lived since the revolutionary war and where do you now live?

Answer I was living in what is now Lincoln County, State of North Carolina, when called into service. Have lived since in Burke County in that state and now live in Haywood County.

Question 4th   How were you called into service? Were you drafted? Did you volunteer or were you a substitute.

Answer The first tour I served as a volunteer. The other two I was drafted.

Question 5th   State the names of some of the regular officers who were with the troops when you served such continental militia regiments as you recollect and the general commanders of your service.

Answer I knew none of the regular officers, there being none with the troops I served with, nor was I with any continental regiment as I now believe, nor have I a distinct recollection of the militia regiments I served with. All the time I served was against the Indians, except the first tour against the Tories.

Question 6th   Did you ever receive a discharge from service? If so, from whom was it given? What has become of it?

Answer I received none for the first two tours. The last I received one from Captain Daniel Smith.

Question 7th   State the names of persons to whom you are known in your present neighborhood and who can testify as to your character for veracity and their belief of your service as a soldier of the revolution.

Answer I am acquainted with Jacob Fulbright and Andrew Shook, there being no clergyman in my neighborhood with whom I am acquainted who has knowledge of my revolutionary character.

He hereby relinquishes any claim whatever to a pension or annuity except the present and declares that his name is not on the pension roll of the agency of any state.

Sworn to & subscribed
in open court the   Jacob Shook
day & year aforesaid.

Wm Johnston, Clk

We, Jacob Fulbright and Andrew Shook, both residing in the County of Haywood, North Carolina, hereby certify that we are well acquainted with Jacob Shook, who has subscribed & sworn to the above declaration. That we believe him to be eighty-four years of age, that he is _____ & he lived in the neighborhood where he resides, to have been a soldier of the revolution and we concur in that opinion.

Jacob Shook's pension application, page 2

Jacob Shook Revolutionary War Pension Application *Page 3*

Sworn to & subscribed
in open court the
day & year aforesaid.

                                                    his
                                      Jacob X Fulbright
                                                mark

                                                  his
                                      Andrew X Shook
                                                mark

Wm Johnston, Clk

This (following) file was contributed for use in the USGenWeb
Archives by: William R. Navey genealogy1@ancestry.com
===

NORTH CAROLINA
PENSION ROLL
OF 1835
****

REPORT FROM THE SECRETARY OF WAR
IN RELATION TO THE PENSION ESTABLISHMENT
OF THE UNITED STATES
1835

****
COPIED AND INDEXED BY WILLIAM R. NAVEY
P. O. BOX 251
HOLLY RIDGE, NC 28445-0251

REPORT FROM THE SECRETARY OF WAR IN OBEDIENCE TO
RESOLUTIONS OF THE SENATE OF THE 5TH AND 30TH OF JUNE, 1834
AND THE 3RD OF MARCH, 1835

IN RELATION TO PENSION ESTABLISHMENT OF THE UNITED STATES
****
ORIGINALLY PUBLISHED AS
UNITED STATES GOVERNMENT DOCUMENTS
SERIAL NUMBERS 249, 250, 251
SENATE DOCUMENT 514
****
WASHINGTON
PRINTED BY DUFF GREEN 1835

**JACOB SHOOK
HAYWOOD COUNTY
PRIVATE
NORTH CAROLINA MILITIA
$20.00 ANNUAL ALLOWANCE
$60.00 AMOUNT RECEIVED
DECEMBER 20, 1833 PENSION STARTED
AGE 85**

Jacob Shook's pension application, page 3

Jacob Shook's only known signature

I must give credit for this Revolutionary War chapter to our deceased cousin, Bob Jones, who wrote the majority of this text in 2001 for the www.shookhistory.org website.] Bob had a photographic memory, and was able to remember all that he had ever read and studied. He loved history and had a broad knowledge of all the history surrounding him. Bob loved this time period and knew it well. He especially loved the history of North Carolina. I do not have such knowledge, nor do I have the sources to go find it. I believe that Bob would approve of the way his work has been used for this book. He too, was proud to be a Shook kid.

JACOB AFTER THE WAR

The Revolution came to an end in 1783, and in that same year, Jacob appears once more. In a case brought before the confiscation courts meeting in Lincoln County, he and two others presented a charge against a man from Lyle's Creek. They accused the man of supporting the king during the war.

The court refused to return an indictment as the evidence was lacking, so the man went unpunished. Unknown is the source of this bit of information, other than it appears in the minutes of that unusual court. It was cited as an example of the actions taken against Tories by the new American government and how uncharacteristically reasonable and forgiving these courts were on the frontier of North Carolina.

Oddly enough, dealing with the Tories came closer to home a few years later.

Peter Yount, Jacob's first cousin, had served in the Revolutionary War along with Jacob and brother Andrew in some actions. Peter was accused of having sympathies with the Tories, and he lost land that he had been granted by a warrant as pay for some of his service time. We can see Peter's side and understand, to a point, how he felt. He was a German immigrant who was aided by the English to immigrate to the colonies. It was traditional that all immigrants swear an oath of allegiance to the British Empire when they debarked from the ships on reaching American ports.

Peter felt much gratitude to the English for the help given to him.

So here and there, we see the shadow of the individual man Jacob has become, and we can see a fuzzy vision of him with his thick German accent, frontier garb, and plain ways. We see a landholder, a juror, a man willing to seek redress in court, and a churchgoer. We see a veteran patriot, an Indian fighter, and, most of all, a pioneer since his teens. Beyond that, all the rest of his early life is obscured by the mists of time that envelope him.

Even more undetectable with our meager means are the reasons for Jacob's move from his large extended family established on Lyle's Creek to the mountains of western North Carolina.

We have learned from the Revolutionary War archives that at one time, Rutherford's troops were camped on the banks of the Pigeon River. Jacob and Andrew were together on this assignment.

> "Here, Rutherford again waited for some time as he sent scouts deeper into Cherokee country, and they waited for supplies to reach them. The area where some of Rutherford's troops waited would later become Clyde, North Carolina, and we can imagine Jacob and Andrew as they took in its wonders. They probably hunted the nearby hills of the Newfound [Mountain] range and fished the crystal waters of the Pigeon River and determined that when all this was over, they would return to this paradise

spot. And they did, ten years later, to live and raise families."

His marriage to Isabella Weitzel is still shrouded in much mystery. Many genealogy researchers have theories, but they are just that, theories, and ours is among them. History has not revealed any details of how and where they met. In the matter of his matrimony, some questions need be asked. Who was this Isabella? There are listings of his marriage dating from as early as 1770. Were they married in Lincoln County, North Carolina? There were several Weitzel families living in the same Pennsylvania community as the Shooks. No recording of their marriage can be found anywhere, but many German unions weren't recorded in that day, and many, many records had been lost. We know that Jacob Fulbright was married to Elizabeth Weitzel before that family moved to North Carolina. Was Isabella there too? Were they sisters? Did Isabella reside in Catawba County with the Shook extended families during the war? There is a Jacob Weitzel in the records as an early settler of Buncombe County. Was he a brother? He was from Lincoln County, which would seem to indicate a connection. Looking further, we find Weitzel families centered in both Orange and Guilford Counties, North Carolina, who were descendants of Henrich Weitzel, who moved to North Carolina from Augusta County, Virginia, before 1770. This family eventually Americanized the name to *Wiesel*. Interestingly, there is some indication that Jacob and Isabella married in Guilford County. When and where were their first children born? Records indicate that John, Abraham, Daniel, Jacob Jr., Susannah, and Elizabeth were born before 1780. These and many other questions are still without answers clothed in these mists of time, and these answers are not for us to know now. One thing we are certain of is that they were married for [approximately] sixty-five to seventy years and that they raised eleven children to adulthood. This is the only thing that really matters to us today.

The 1790 Census
Jacob Shuke/Shook, 1st Co,
Morgan Dist. Burke County, NC

Males age 16+	1
Males under 16	6
Total females	3
Slaves	0

Note: This would have been Jacob and his sons Jacob Jr., John, Abraham, Daniel, David, and probably Peter, as his birth date is 29 October 1790. The females would be Isabella, Susanna, and Elizabeth. Jacob was still under contract with the new federal government in 1790 when the first census was taken by the military to serve its own purpose.

Had he taken refuge there near old Fort Davidson during the Indian troubles of that year? Or had he, as others say, only moved to the foot of the mountains by 1790 and not on to the Pigeon River? I think it is easy to believe both. Often, settlers would find a piece of land they wanted and spend years improving the land in anticipation of a later grant. Since Jacob never owned land on Lyle's Creek, it seems that he might well have spent the winters in a slightly more established and safer area with friends and taken his family to help work his new claim in the mountains during the summer months. It is interesting that adjacent or close by to Jacob in the 1790 enumeration lived Joseph McPeters, who also laid claim to being the Pigeon River's earliest settler, along with several other Revolutionary War soldiers that would have been known to Jacob Shook.

The 1800 Census
Jacob Shook, Buncombe Co, NC
Buncombe had been cut from Burke
and Rutherford 5 December 1791

Age	Males	Females
45 +	1	0
26 to 45	0	1
16–26	2	1
10–16	1	0
0–10	2	3
Slaves	0	0

The 1810 Census
Jacob Shook, Haywood County, North Carolina
Haywood County was cut from Buncombe 15
December 1808

Age	Males	Females
45+	1	0
16–26	2	0
Slaves	0	0

All the females and the younger males were missing from Jacob's household in 1810. They were back in 1820. In 1810, Haywood County was still wild, primitive, and lawless. With the unrest that led to the War of 1812 already in evidence, perhaps they moved back off the frontier to safer territory. Interestingly, there was in Lincoln County, North Carolina, a William Shook household headed by a male no more than sixteen years old and an older female. However, please remember that there is no known record of Jacob having a son named William.

The 1820 Census
Jacob Shook, Haywood County, North Carolina

Age	Males	Females
45+	1	1
16–26	0	1
0–10	0	1
Slaves	0	0

The 1830 Census
Jacob Shook, Haywood County, North Carolina

Age	Males	Females
80–90	1	0 Jacob age 81
70–80	0	1 Isabella age
70–75		
20–30	1	0
10–15	0	1
Slaves	0	0

Both Jacob and Isabella had passed away prior to the 1840 census.

TAKING UP RESIDENCE ON THE PIGEON RIVER

Long-held oral tradition says that Jacob first came to settle on the Pigeon River at Clyde, North Carolina, in 1786. This would have made him one of the very first settlers in the area, a position of honor that we find jealously defended by other families even to this day. However, it is not this easy. There is no documentation for the year that Jacob moved his family into this valley. The county boundaries were constantly being redrawn. Courthouses were sometimes several days' distant from where a family lived; records were lost. There were many reasons why records seemed so haphazardly kept in the early days.

Ideal documentation or not, Jacob does have his family settling in his valley where he put down his roots and lived the remainder of his life. The first thing we need to address is, how did he get to settle on the west side of the Pigeon River?

Some of this confusion might be explained by the particular status of the valley of the Pigeon River in relation to the Cherokee. This was a very turbulent time for the Cherokee nation. They had been used by the English and the French governments in the past decades and pitted against white settlers for the gain of these two governments. Treaties were made and quickly broken on every hand. It is little wonder that few Cherokee people had any faith in the words and promises from the white man's government. It is necessary here to get some background from the Cherokee nation's position.

They had sued for peace in 1771 and signed the Big Pigeon Treaty at Long Island of the Holston River in Tennessee. In the treaty, the Indians gave North Carolina "all the lands east of the Pigeon River." The government of North Carolina agreed to pay for this land. After the treaty, it was discovered that none of the signatures had the rights of ownership to that parcel, so the Cherokee nation declared that portion of the treaty null and void. Thus the area west of the Blue Ridge on to the Pigeon River, which today is in Buncombe County and the eastern part of Haywood County, became "the disputed territories." Due to this dispute, North Carolina closed the territory to all settlements.

North Carolina was financially bankrupt after the lengthy Revolutionary War and found it not only unable to pay the Cherokee nation for the land beyond the Blue Ridge as they had promised, but was also under great pressure from creditors, including its unpaid veterans, to come up with cash. To this end, in 1783, the state of North Carolina announced the disputed land on the *east* side of the Pigeon River to be open for grant and settlement. Land on the west side of the Pigeon River, where Jacob settled, was still closed for white settlement and in the hands of the Cherokee nation.

The early settlers of this mountain section generally made friends with the Indians upon arriving there. And some of the white settlers greatly befriended the Cherokee people. One early settler, Edward Hyatt, was seeing much of his Cherokee neighbors. As well-established tradition has it, the Indians often visited in the home of Mr. and Mrs. Hyatt; he would invite them to put their feet under the table, and it appears that Mrs. Hyatt would also give them food in case her husband was away from home.

One unproven theory is that Hyatt may have begun selling land after the Revolution and that Jacob may have acquired his original tract from Hyatt, as did others. Haywood County had not yet been formed from Buncombe and Burke Counties. In the ensuing confusion, many deeds were never recorded or had been lost.

Let us look at another theory. Family lore and traditional stories were handed down through the generations without proven documentation. However, they are too frequent and similar to be completely ignored. Jacob was a friend to the Cherokee people. Jacob also made friends with the local bands of the Cherokee people whenever possible. Jacob could also have obtained his land from the Cherokee Chief Junalaska who had opened his lands for white settlement in 1789.

Robert Shook, descended from Frederick, who was a younger brother to Jacob, has written the story about his Shook line in *A Journey in Courage*. In this book, we learn that Jacob had an early encounter with a young Cherokee mother hiding with her infant son amid some thick undergrowth during a fierce battle between the North Carolina militia and a band of renegade Cherokee. The infant was missing a hand. When Jacob realized that she posed no danger to him, he quickly motioned for her to be quiet and remain where she was, as he backed away from her. Several years later, Jacob was to meet up with this same Cherokee mother and her son. The seed of a lifelong friendship between the families was sown. Throughout the rest of his life, Jacob offered friendship and substance to this small band of Cherokee people, and they did the same to him. The families mingled, visiting in each other's homes, sharing the yield of crops, and going on hunting forays. This friendship culminated in the marriage between a beautiful Cherokee maiden and a beloved Shook son who was descended from Frederick.

After Jacob died, a precious tomahawk was sold in his estate sale. This is all the proof we need to know that Jacob did indeed have a special friendship with his Cherokee neighbors. It is not so hard to believe that he had their permission to settle his family on land still under their control. This could be the reason why no deed or grant of any kind has ever been found for the land where he built his houses, raised his family, and lived upon the rest of his life. Nothing happens by just sheer luck. This was where God wanted Jacob to be.

How and exactly when he settled where he did is something that belongs to history and is not for us to know. We must take the evidence as seen. He was there, and there was where his life took another turn that made it stand apart so that we know of him two hundred years later and are thankful for the legacy that he gave to his many thousands of descendants.

LIFE ON THE PIGEON RIVER

Jacob had now firmly secured land on the west side of the Pigeon River. He had built the first house to provide shelter for the growing family. This house would adequately serve his family for the first years while they were establishing their farm. He was beginning in earnest to build not only a residence but also his homestead. The site he chose to build their home was located less than a quarter of a mile from the Pigeon River. The land sloped gently down to the river. There was a fair-sized branch, or small a creek, running through the land he had chosen. It ran fast and clear water from a higher elevation in the mountains to the west of this valley. It would provide all the clean water his family and his stock would ever need. This little stream was one of many that fed into the Pigeon River. It is flowing down to the river today. All one need do to find the place of their first home is follow this little stream of water from the river on past the big house and highway south for a thousand yards or so. A beautiful modern home sits there now in the upper right-hand corner of an intersection. This is about equal distance as the big house is from the river.

German people were known for their hard work, extending for long hours, with every moment filled with productivity. There were no idle times, day or night, for the family. Children had chores to do from gathering eggs and feeding chickens to more labor-intensive work for the older children. Their time would not be all work with no play, for there was fishing in the Pigeon River, trapping rabbits, and hunting for larger game in the woods that surrounded them. The children viewed their catch as prizes that were used as food for the family. Animal skins were tanned and softened so that they may be used for items of clothing, shoes, and boots. Wild berries and herbs were to be found in the thick woods around them. Gathering these may have been done by the younger children and the older daughters accompanied by whoever was available among the older brothers who acted as guides and guards. The danger of roving bands of rogue young Cherokees was ever present. The young Cherokees may have been tempted to interfere with the children and daughters as they went about their picking and gathering. However, they would hesitate to take on an older brother who carried some kind of weapon.

There was urgency in building enough shelters and sheds for a growing collection of farm animals. There were horses, of course, oxen, cows, and goats to provide milk, butter, and cheese. Split-rail fences were put in place to corral the larger animals. Isabella's herd of sheep was of utmost importance to provide wool for spinning and weaving the large family's clothing.

These were the busiest of times. There were only a few other families in this valley and in the community at this time. Workers for hire were few. Jacob missed the help of his large extended family who were still living on Lyle's Creek in Catawba County. So much had to be done before the winter set in.

Huge spaces were laid out and prepared for the kitchen garden, where all manner of vegetables, herbs, berries, and flowers would be planted. Seeds and cuttings had been carefully collected and hoarded. Orchards were planted to provide fruit. Fields were cleared and prepared for the coming planting season. Corn, oats, rye, and wheat would be planted for the family's use and to feed the animals. This was a time the whole family felt a sense of fulfillment. With the passing of every day, everyone could see the family's dream coming true. There was joy in their hearts when they saw a blacksmith shop being built among the many other buildings and sheds.

Still, time was made for resting, for lessons in reading, writing, math, and, most of all, for God and for prayers of thanksgiving. Every morning, while the family ate their first meal of the day, was a time for family devotion and prayer as Jacob read a few scriptures from the old German Bible he had obtained in his earliest adult years. This was a time of encouragement and praise for each of the family members, especially the children, as they went about the day's business.

Fire Guts Shook House At Clyde

6A - The MOUNTAINEER, Waynesville, N.C. Wednesday, October 2, 1974
The Jacob Shook house at Clyde, estimated to be 200 years old, was gutted by fire Tuesday morning. Cause of the fire was attributed to a faulty flue.

The house - built of logs and in later years covered with weather boarding and paneled inside - was occupied by Mr. and Mrs. Dewey Metcalf.

The Metcalfs were outside working when Mrs. Metcalf went back to the house for something and smelled smoke. She called to her husband, and together they looked for signs of smoke or fire. They found smoke coming from behind paneling where the flue is located.

The Shook house is situated about a quarter of a mile off US 19 in Caldwell Cove west of town. A neighbor saw smoke coming from the house and reported to the Clyde Fire Department. Assisting were Center Pigeon and North Canton Beaverdam Volunteer Fire departments and Canton, which sent a water tanker.

The inside of the house was gutted and the outside porch and roof were heavily damaged.

Fire guts *first* Shook house in Clyde

This newspaper article and picture of the first house Jacob built for his family was located less than a quarter of a mile from the west banks of the Pigeon River. It was located about a thousand yards south of the site for the big house and beside the little stream of water that served all their needs. This first house was built of logs and was later covered with weatherboarding.

The house was small in the beginning, but would be enlarged a number of times in the coming years.

There is a widely published story that Jacob built the big house for his son Peter; however, this story is totally false. This is the first house that Jacob built for his family when the family first came into this valley. It served Jacob's family well for a few of years. After the big house was completed, Jacob sold this first house to Peter. This was where Peter lived and raised his large family. This is the house with six acres of land that Jacob sold to son Peter for twelve dollars on December 25, 1836. A copy of the original deed transferring six acres with this house from Jacob to Peter can be found in the book of deeds of the Haywood County courthouse, book C, pages 384 and 385. This home would be known as Mahala's house until her death on March 6, 1894. She lived here with their children for twenty-nine years after Peter's death. She and two unmarried daughters lived on in their home long after the other children had grown, married, and moved into their own homes.

A NEW SPIRIT AND A NEW HOME

The Shook family had settled into the routine of normal daily life on their farm. Everyone took part in doing whatever needed to be done. After chores and lessons were completed, they would go fishing, or maybe they would hitch up a cart and go visiting with their mother. Isabella often visited the sick and helped new mothers.

There were no organized churches in this rapidly growing community. Folks did receive visits from a circuit rider from time to time. A circuit rider was a minister who traveled over the land on horseback and served small communities and single families who were isolated in this still very wild country. These ministers performed marriages, sometimes long after the couple had established a home and started a family. They also preached and baptized all who wished to be baptized. These circuit riders would lend a hand at manual labor whenever they were needed to help raise a barn, build a fence, or whatever else was needed. They always read the scriptures and prayed with all whom they met if the other party was agreeable. They also knew a good deal of doctoring, having with them a supply of simple herbs and knowledge of how to use them for healing purposes. They usually stayed with a family for a few days, often sleeping in the hayloft of a barn.

One such minister was the Reverend Henry Boehm. Reverend Boehm may have been the first that Jacob heard speaking of the new Methodist religion. Jacob missed going to church with his parents and the extended family. He had done so all his life back in Pennsylvania and in Catawba County, so he looked forward to the times when Reverend Boehm would be in their midst. Jacob had built a large barn with a threshing floor for the grain he grew each year. He had offered the use of the barn to Reverend Boehm. The threshing floor made a wonderful place to have service. It was large enough to accommodate several persons. The barn was always dry, and it was warmer in winter than the outdoors.

Still, there was a hole in Jacob's heart that nothing he did could fill. He just knew that there was something lacking in his life. Something was missing that neither his family, his farm, nor his friends could provide.

> The Reverend T. F. Glenn tells us about this event in Jacob's life in his book *History of Methodism*.
>
> Shook was powerfully converted after the old fashion Methodist style. Whilst under deep conviction for sin, he went out into the cornfield to plow. He prayed and wept as he worked. Finally the burden of guilt was lifted and his soul was flooded with joy. He shouted and praised the LORD as He continued to work. He dropped the lines, left his plow, lost his hat, and shouted all over the field. That was a happy, triumphant day for the new convert; but the horse played havoc with the corn.

This is the one event that changed Jacob's life far more than anything he had ever experienced or would experience. Finally, his heart and soul were filled with joy, and he felt complete. Jacob henceforth lived his life for God. Every deed was done with the desire in his heart to follow the pathway led by Jesus Christ, the Son of the Living God. Now his life's work had truly begun. All that he had been taught, all that he had learned, all that he had done as a Revolutionary War patriot, as an Indian fighter with the North Carolina militia, all that he was as a husband, father, son, friend, and neighbor only served to prepare him to serve his God and his Lord Jesus Christ.

THE BUILDING BEGINS

Tradition tells us that Jacob began to build his dream home around 1795. He thought about building this house as he went about his work. This was the home he had built in his mind so many times over the years in that beautiful valley. He had planned it all in his mind and sketched it on any scrap of paper he could find, as well as on the back of tanned skins, and even in the dirt beside his campfires. He had many long discussions about it with Isabella, his beloved wife, and with his grown sons. This would be no small log cabin that could be built within a few days' time. Jacob wanted a grand house where he would have space for visitors as well as a comfortable home for his growing family. He and his sons began cutting the trees and bringing them to the home site. He had selected the best trees to be cut and prepared. He wanted the very best virgin timber available that grew on his land. He would choose chestnut, and white oak trees for the support beams, floors, and walls. These were strong woods that would resist rot and insect damage over the years. These beams and walls have remained solid for more than two hundred years and continue so unto this day in 2012.

He had chosen this site about halfway between their first home and the Pigeon River. It would also be built close to the same stream of water that was providing clean, sweet water for all their needs. His barns, barn lots, and his many storage buildings, along with his blacksmith's shop, would lie between the houses, near this stream of water. This stream was fenced so that the animals could not pollute the water. The children kept water troughs filled for them.

He wanted this house to be of service to his Lord, just as he did for everything that was now in his life. So Jacob began to plan a third floor to his already-remarkable house plans. He wanted to build a place that would be used only for religious purposes, a place that would be dedicated to the service of God. He would build a house with four rooms over four rooms, with stacked staircases in the middle of the house that would go up to all three floors. He wanted a large wide porch where they would sit and share conversation with friends and visitors to his home.

The kitchen would be built in a separate structure, detached from the main house for safety reasons. Kitchen fires were always a concern. The kitchen would be spacious, with enough room for the family to have their meals around a large table with many chairs. It would also have a large pantry and be connected to the root cellar and smokehouse where all their food supplies were stored.

Jacob would build his house by the post-and-beam method that he had learned in his childhood from his grandfather Johannes Schuck, who in turn had learned this method of building houses in Germany, the old country. This made a stout building, one that could stand the howling winter winds that blew down the side of the mountains and through the valley. This method entailed much hard work. It was a slow and painstaking handwork using a chisel and a hammer. He would notch out holes through the timbers that other chiseled timber ends would fit into. Then he would peg the two beams together so that they could never move. A prime example of this can still be seen today in the white oak main support beam under the house.

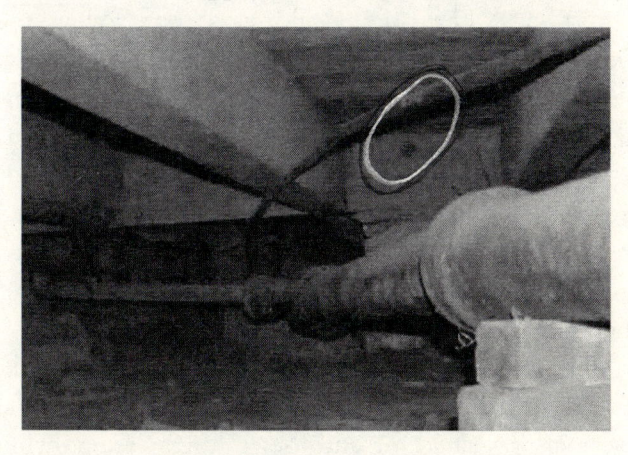

The pegged main support beam underneath the house

There were no sawmills at this time. The massive logs were cut into boards using the pit sawing method. Two men were required to do this. One man would be down in the pit, and the other at the top, and they would push-pull a long saw blade back and forth to split off slabs of planking from the logs. These saw marks are very visible on the wide boards throughout the house today.

Jacob had already been making nails in his blacksmith's shop by cutting square iron rods to desired length and hammering a sharp point on each nail. There are countless numbers of these nails still to be found in the house. There is one place where they can be found in abundance. This is in the chapel room, behind the wall near the corner adjoining the window wall and the stair wall. They are protruding through a portion of the original shingled roof. When the Smathers family enlarged the house, they extended a new roof over part of Jacob's old wood shake roof. This has sheltered the old wood shingles from the ravages of time and weather. During the latest renovation this area was area was filled in with new boards and sealed from view. I sincerely hope this area will be uncovered and a then sealed with Plexiglas someday. It is one of the most interesting displays of artifacts in the house.

This certainly was a busy time for the Shook family. The farmlands were improved and expanded, the livestock was cared for, and the children were growing up demanding more of their father's time and attention. Jacob still visited his Cherokee friends to make sure that they were well and that their needs were supplied.

The building of the new house was the daily focus for the family. It required all the help that could be assembled each day from youths and adults alike. There was enough work for all, and more. The community was growing at a rapid pace as new families moved into the valley. New neighbors had their own building to do, and finding time to help Jacob from time to time was difficult. Nevertheless, help did come. Word of mouth about this mansion being built spread throughout Western North Carolina, and men wanted to be a part of it. They came and offered their labor for a day, for a week, for whatever time they could spare from their own work at home. As the house took shape, walls went up, and as the magnificence of it all became apparent, even more people came to work as much and as long as they could. They brought their wives, who were just as interested in this wonderful house as the men were. The women gathered and prepared meals for the working men. Older children also wanted to join Jacob's own sons in doing what they could. Jacob's Cherokee friends were often there, working alongside the others.

Jacob was equally busy with his work for God. He never missed an opportunity to witness about Jesus. Work breaks were always a brief time to read the scripture and pray with all who were in attendance. New families moved into the valley. They had already heard of the Methodist movement from the circuit riders and were overjoyed at finding Jacob as a neighbor. They became regular attendees in all worship services. They were faithful to lend a hand with the building as often as possible. They were thrilled with the attic room that would become their place of worship.

HOUSE CELEBRATION AND THE ORGANIZATION OF A NEW METHODIST CONGREGATION

In the year of our Lord 1798, the house was finally finished. Jacob and his family were so pleased with the results for the house exceeded their dreams. There were glass panes in all of the windows. In more modest log cabins oiled paper was hung at the windows. The family could look out at any window at all that surrounded them. To the North was the Pigeon River that supplied fresh fish for their dinner table. Looking to the South, one would see their barn lots, animal pens, and an assortment of farm buildings. Jacob's blacksmith shop was there. Everything was close to the little steam of water that supplied animals and the family with cold spring water. To the West, one would see all the kitchen gardens and orchards. To the East lay Jacob's cultivated fields. He had amassed some 1500 acres that covers most all of the ground where the city of Clyde is today. Yes, they were proud and thankful to God for all of his countless blessings on them. Indeed, his cup was running over. Jacob and all the settlers around him were prospering.

This was a happy time, and a weeklong housewarming celebration was being planned. In our mind's eye and in our hearts, we can share this special celebration. News and invitations had gone out to all the communities in Western North Carolina. Meat was butchered, fish were caught and dried, the children were busy gathering nuts and berries. Honey was gathered from hives in the woods. Women spent countless hours cooking and baking. Much food would be needed during the weeklong celebration. Not only the Shook women were cooking, but all women who would be coming were preparing food to take to share at the celebration. The extended family from Catawba County was coming, so the celebration would be a family reunion as well.

Many ministers of all denominations, including all the circuit preachers and Reverend Henry Boehm, were coming. The farmers were almost finished with laying in the crops for the year, so whole families would come from all the neighboring communities. Jacob, his older sons, and the local men were busy building a brush arbor. Seating was fashioned from logs and a simple podium would be built for the speakers. Campsites were laid out for the tents and wagons for each family coming. Enclosures for all the visitor's horses, mules, and milk cows were made.

This was such a special time. There would be days of singing, sermons, and sharing fellowship with one another. The dedication service, giving the attic room to God, was to be done early in the celebration. A new Methodist church was to be organized, and it would be the first organized Methodist church in the state of North Carolina. No records of the early membership have survived. All of this was recorded in heaven, and that is enough for us today.

This attic room, closest room to heaven, was ready. Some called it the Chapel Room. It now had split logs for seating and a pulpit. Pegs along one side were fixed to hold coats and hats. The room would be filled to standing room only, mostly with men. One reason there were more men than women present on this day is simply that there were many more men in the valley than there were women and children. Several of the men were unmarried because they choose to established a farm and home before marrying and beginning a family. Many men choose to leave their wives and children behind in a safe and sheltered fort while they established a place for them.

Women and children would hear the sermons and songs drifting down into the rest of the house. The two windows would be open, and those people sitting on the ground around the house could also hear. Visiting preachers would begin a tradition that would last for decades; they would write their names and the date of their visit on the wall between the windows in the chapel room. These names are still there today, barely visible, but there. They are now protected by a sheet of Plexiglas. The earliest that can be read is dated 1804.

The weeklong celebration was a great success. It filled a great social and religious need that was lacking in the scattered and isolated communities of Western North Carolina. This gathering started a tradition that was to be carried on for the rest of Jacob's life. These gatherings would be called *Campground Meetings*, and they would be held annually. The Chapel Room would continue to be used as a meeting place for services and worshipping of God some 42 years until both Isabella and Jacob had passed away. This church would later be named Louisa Chapel, and it still exists, very much alive, today in Clyde, North Carolina.

HOW THE HOUSE WAS USED IN JACOB'S TIME

The house was more than a family home for the rest of Jacob's life. The newly organized church met there several times each week. The house was used mightily in spreading Methodism throughout Western North Carolina in the first four decades of its existence. Some of the earliest Methodist preaching in Haywood County took place in and around this house.

There are many, many publications telling us about how the house was used during Jacob's lifetime and after to this day. The local newspapers' archives would prove to be rich places to research for stories of early to recent events in our time.

A few of the early writers that tell us about the work that was done here are W. C. Allen's *Early History of Haywood County*, T. F. Glenn in his *History of Methodism*, W. C. Medford's many writings, and the writings of Bishop M'Kendree and John M'Gee. Bishop Francis Asbury's journals are the most widely known.

Bishops Francis Asbury and Thomas Coke were sent to America by John Wesley to spread the word in an effort to convert new populations. The Methodist church designated a local preacher to a circuit. About a dozen churches would be grouped in a circuit, and ministers toured around to these churches rather than being at one location.

One of these traveling preachers, Bishop Francis Asbury, came through western North Carolina's rugged terrain and kept a journal of his arduous travels, often sharing candid remarks.

> In his journal on page 654, Bishop Asbury himself tells us about a visit to the Shook house.
> On Friday, November 30, 1810 our troubles began at the foaming, roaring stream, which hid the rocks. At Cataloochee, I walked over a log. But O, the mountains...height after height, and five miles over! After crossing other streams, and losing ourselves in the woods, we came in, about nine o'clock at night, to Vater Shook's What an awful day! *Vater* means Father.

This particular story has been the source of much debate as to whether Bishop Asbury preached there or not. The overwhelming consensus is that he did. Bishop Ashbury continues to relate that other companions traveled on the next morning to Samuel Edney's while he and Samuel Boehm went to Asheville where they were to hold services on the Sabbath. That means they could have spent Saturday morning preaching at the Shook's home, an activity that Henry Boehm said they did at every stop.

We can easily visualize that word went out to the community that the Bishop was at the Shook house, and folks gathered. They would have gathered and filled the house and covered the grounds around the house. He very easily could have climbed the stairs to the Chapel Room and have offered a sermon to the gathered audience of family and neighbors.

We also might wonder which child gave up their warm bed to the cold and exhausted Bishop that night. Travelers would have often been an overnight guests. We can well imagine that the hospitable and benevolent Jacob and Isabella kept accommodations ready at all times.

The following newspaper article was found with a collection of other old publications.

The newspaper is unidentified.

> Bishop Asbury Preached in the Attic of Shook House At Clyde In 1810
> By W. C. Medford
> Clyde, April 30, ?
>
> "Jesus lover of my soul, let me to thy bosom fly"... The singing was mostly that of men's voices raised in worship, and unaccompanied by musical instrument. It was in the autumn of 1810 to be exact. November 30; and the place, Jacob Shook's residence on Lower Pigeon River, now Clyde in Haywood County.
>
> Bishop Francis Ashbury has arrived at 9 o'clock that evening; exhausted from long hours in the saddle over rough terrain. Perchance his worn, black clerical suit was soiled from the mire of the road. Word had been dispatched to the neighbors round about that Ashbury was to preach either that afternoon or night – as was his custom to preach everywhere he went.

So the good Bishop, now feeling nourished and well rested, was about ready to begin the service.

Jacob Shook, the Bishop's host, had seen to the nourishment and rest. Shook, the thrifty, hospitable German always saw to that—that none who came to his home hungry or in need was neglected. Service is Held. Now as the folks arrive, they secure their nags to the hitching post in front of Brother Shook's house—a commodious home, built here in this semi-wilderness. So spacious is it that the third story attic-room where the meeting is being held could accommodate a fair-sized congregation.

Listen! They have now started, "How firm a foundation"... as the people continued to crowd into the room. "What more can He say than to you He hath said" resounds throughout the building. The volume is such that the crackle of fowl and tinkle of cow bells around Shook's barnyard can scarce be heard.

Ashbury after preaching here...illegible..."

Bishop Asbury seems to have made it clear to those who came to hear him preach in the Shook House attic room and elsewhere that "man does not live by bread alone". Also that it behooves all the faithful to work while it is yet day, as he himself did.

As the record goes, Asbury was sent by John Wesley as a missionary to America in 1770. He was ordained first Bishop of Methodism in the United States in 1784. It is said that he preached seventeen thousand times, traveling meanwhile over many thousand miles on his work in several states, also that he ordained three thousand preachers.

So it was; the good Bishop, when he had "the burning heart" to come this way, had in 1810 one of the first Methodist services to be held in all the territory west of Buncombe County. But we must not forget the hospitable and benevolent Jacob Shook who set aside this chapel room, helping as much to make the good work possible.

Other preachers continued to hold services at the Shook house, so it became a sort of headquarters for Methodism here for a while, it being the forerunner of Shook's Campground Meetings. Many persons were converted in these old-timey meetings, Jacob Shook himself being among them not many years before."

Jacob and Isabella continued to use their home as they had dreamed, being led along this footpath by our LORD. The house had become the center of the Methodist movement in western North Carolina. Friends continued to pour into the home. They came for many reasons. Often they came just to sit and visit and talk over the years shared and remembered together.

REUBEN PHILIPS AT THE SHOOK HOUSE

Rueben Philips was born December 4, 1795, and died February 12, 1887. He was one of those outstanding pioneers as our nation was established and growing so much. Researching and reading about his life is a real pleasure for us. There is much written and published about him. Like Jacob, his life was devoted to his LORD and Savior, Jesus Christ, the Son of the living God.

Reuben was a well-known teacher, preacher, and circuit rider in all the communities of Western North Carolina in the early 1800s. Reuben was the son of Adam Philips, who also was a teacher, a singer, and a Methodist minister. Reuben was a child prodigy of highly unusual talent for learning. He excelled in learning math, reading, writing, and surveying, to name only a few. He spent his life teaching the three Rs—reading, writing, and arithmetic—in subscription schools and teaching music and preaching the gospel.

There were no public schools in the first quarter of the nineteenth century. When a community had enough settlers with children and had the means to hire a teacher for a determined period of time, a contract was drawn up between the community leaders and the teacher. This practice was known as being a subscription school. Room and board was always included in the contract.

Rueben was also a personal friend of Joseph Hicks, who married Margaret Shook in 1817. Rueben posted the one-hundred-dollar marriage bond for them when they married. Through this connection, Jacob was well aware of Rueben and his work.

The Biography of Rueben Philips, written by descendant Wesley Philips and contains material written by Rueben in his journals. Rueben tells this story therein.

My good success was published all over the county and a petition was sent from Locust Old Fields where I had before taught school for me to teach a reading school and a singing school for them. That was violently opposed by the community of Sandymush but by getting me to promise to return to them they gave up, so I opened a school at Locust Old Fields on the first Monday of January 1818 and a music school also for Saturdays and Sundays gratuitously.

Rueben Philips wrote that old Father Jacob Shook "came to hear us sing and was so delighted that he proposed his house for me to sing in, being five miles from where I was teaching."

Sometime in 1818 Rueben Philips opened a music school in the Jacob Shook home. Philips graphically described part of the shook house. "Old Father Shook had a fine house and in the third story had a room 40 feet square, (an over estimation) all finished off in good style which was a room he had well seated for preaching room for he was a Methodist...So I made a large school at that place, some fifty scholars."

While teaching music at the Shook house, Philips often had the assistance of his old friend, Humphrey Posey, who was also an experienced teacher of music. Rueben Philips wrote of the music school at the Jacob shook house:

"The Shook house drew together a vast concourse of young people from both schools, Locust Old Fields included. Toward the end of the summer my friends Posey and Parson

Byers requested that we call all the Sandymush and Newfound music scholars and unite the two schools, and have a three day singing, two days at Father Shook's and one day on Sunday at Waynesville. Waynesville being five miles further west being the county seat and that he, Humphrey Posey, would preach a sermon suited to the occasion which he was well calculated to do. The schools accordingly met and Posey and Vinson Edmonson, both old teachers, were in attendance and some over 120 singers and we had the greatest singing ever witnessed in that county. On Sunday we went to the courthouse at Waynesville and at 12 o'clock we closed the singing and went in procession to the Muster Field where a stand was erected for preaching. The hymn was sung that affects my heart. I was so overcome as to be scarcely able to stand. The hymn was commenced, "Oh tell me no more of this worlds vain store."

This story is also included in the book *May We All Remember Well*, edited by Robert S. Brunk.

SHOOK'S CAMPGROUND MEETINGS

Campground Meetings may have had their birth when the surrounding communities came together to celebrate the finished Shook house with its large Chapel Room designated as a place of worship. The newly formed Methodist church, recorded as being organized there in 1798, would have acted as co-host with Jacob and helping with the logistics of hosting for a week a large gathering of people.

>T. F. Glenn in his *History of Methodism* describes the campground meetings this way:
>
>Now it seems that Jacob Shook, who was noted for his industry and zeal in everything he undertook to do, went about the business of service in the field of Christian faith with the same zeal. He set aside acreage not far from his home for a camp meeting ground, the first to be established in this county.
>
>In the early days the camp meeting was a wonderful institution. Shook's Campground was a great rallying place for the Methodist clans, and hundreds of souls were converted there. The plan of the camp ground was interesting. There were about forty tents. Some 'tenters' built neatly framed and weather-boarded tents; others built cottages of round logs. Scaffolds

built on the inside walls served for beds. The dirt floors were carpeted with straw.

A large tent for worship was built in the center of a square plot of ground, which would accommodate a vast assembly. Slabs from a sawmill were used for seats. Then, those who had tents covered the space enclosed by a tent with fresh-cut wheat straw, on this, the penitents could kneel without soiling their clothes.

About daylight the first trumpet was sounded as a signal for the people to rise and prepare for worship. In about half an hour the second trumpet sounded, summoning the people to family prayer in their tents; and the third trumpet sound was for public prayer meeting under the big tent. Then there was preaching….at eight and eleven a.m., three p.m. and at 'early' candlelight.

In those days the men and women were not allowed to sit in church together. Upon entering, the men went to the left of the aisle, the women went to the right. This custom was kept up for a century or longer here, especially in the rural sections. Up until World War 1, there were rural churches with a 'men's side' and 'women's side' of the aisle.

Brother T. F. Glen continued to explain the preparations for the meeting.

"Beginning along about the first week in August, these "seasons of refreshing" lasted generally from two to three weeks. Preparations for this occasion were never overlooked. Folks in every community went over the clothes and mended, cleaned up, cooked and prepared food. Maybe a young hog, veal or mutton was slaughtered and fish caught and dried or salted. Certainly the tents or wagon covers were mended as needed."

Indeed, folks looked forward to this annual camp meeting occasion with such interest that it was generally looked upon as "God's appointed time." And why not? It was a time of leisure, generally when they could rest from their earthly labors. Wheat, oat, and rye had been threshed and corn gathered and stored. Fences had been mended, to keep stock where they belonged. Maybe a ditch bank that needed some attention had been shored up.

But some of these things could wait, for it was "Camp Meeting time!" The old arbor had been cleaned up, the rough board seats or benches put in place, and the earthen floor renewed with fresh straw.

And, of course, brother Bill would again be there and probably Cousin Mack from a more distant community and they hadn't seen one another since last Camp Meeting. No, siree! Aside from the spiritual uplift to be gained at these meetings, the 'powerful sermons' to be heard, the shouting, etc., there were other reasons why a-body just couldn't afford to miss them.

These camp meetings became a religious and social event each year. It was a time of celebration in the fall after crops were harvested. People came from all parts of Western North

Carolina. They came by the hundreds, some say by the thousands.

Jacob selected a central place that would serve as the central meeting place. It is on the side of a small hill, and it has a small swift running spring fed creek at the bottom. This would provide water for all the people and to the dozens and dozens of horses used as a means of transportation and to pull family wagons. Camp space was set up; spaces lain out locations for families to make their camp for the week. Tents and other means of shelter, sometimes under the family wagon, were used. Some families even constructed a semi-permanent wooden shelter that they used year after year.

A speaker's podium, and seating would have been prepared under a brush arbor. There must be provisions for the management and disposal of all the animal and human waste. This task alone must have been horrendous. Some type of schedule for each days event's would be established. There would be time for prayers, singing, preaching, a time for private meetings of the elders. There would be time for men's activities, a time for the women to cook and prepare meals, a time for children's play.

This was a time for all manner of religious services to be conducted, not only singing of hymns and preaching of sermons and prayer meetings, but also weddings and baptisms. It is recorded that Samuel Edney received his ordination as elder in the Methodist church there in 1814. Samuel Edney was the early pastor of the Louisa Chapel.

There was the social side of such gatherings. Buying, selling, and bartering for all manner of goods would be done. Friends would be made, perhaps even lost, and courtships would flourish. Marriages would be arranged, not only among the young but also among the widows and widowers. This mass of people gathered together in one place must have reminded Jacob of his days in the Revolutionary War.

TIME PASSES ON AND HISTORY IS MADE.

Jacob's son, David, took over the religious leadership role in the church after Jacob became too advanced in age to carry on the responsibilities. David blew a horn to call folks to the scheduled services. David blew his horn for these meetings the last time when he was ninety-five years old. He had blown his horn for fifty-one consecutive years. [Could his horn have been a Shofar, made of a ram's horn that the Jews, and all of Abraham's Seed, have always used? They performed the same task of calling the people to worship. Would it be possible for his descendants to locate his horn after all this time?]

As one visits the historical seat of the Shook family's roots, everyone will want to go and see Louisa Chapel. As you stand on the edge of the road, let your mind's eye wonder down the slopping land to see the history of this spot, see the little stream of water that served the needs of all people and their stock during all these Campground Meetings. Let your heart hear the sermons and singing. Most of all, listen for the horn.

In 1835, Jacob gave the four acres of land to the Methodist Church where the Campground Meeting had been held for four decades.

He knew he did not have many more years to live in his valley, and that after he was gone, the house would be sold. Thus this would be the end of his attic Chapel Room being used for worship. He wanted to make sure the congregation had a place to build a new church building. We find in the Haywood County, North Carolina, Records of Deeds Book C, page number 536, this record:

Witnesses Presents, reviewed and ordered to be registered. Certified at office the 10th of April, 1837. William Welch Registered the 15th day of May 1837. B. [?] [?]. This indenture made the 12th day of December in the year of our lord One thousand Eight Hundred and Thirty Five Between Jacob Shook of the County of Haywood N.C. one part and the [?] [?] [?] David Shook, Paxton Ammons, [?] Gibson, Jas Burnett of the other part all of the County and State aforesaid. Witness, that the said Shook doth give unto the said trustees, for the use of the Methodist Council of Churches a certain bit of land in said county including Shook Camp Ground for that purpose. Beginning on west side of the branch [?] a forked [?] on [?] [?] [?] the branch below the spring, then running south 19 degrees East 81 poles to White Oak near the road below the camp ground, then east 20 poles to a [?] Black Ash, then south [?]

poles to a Hickory, then west to the beginning, being four acres 187 poles. I the said Jacob Shook do bind my heirs, assigns, executors, and administrators to the said trustees as long as said land is Required and used by the said Methodist [?] institution whereof in consideration of which I assign, [?] and deliver in presence of [?] [?]

[?]: A. R. Bryant, Peter Shook (Jurat) Jacob Shook (seal)

The current building is the fourth building that the Louisa Chapel has built over the years on this land.

This organized church continued to use the chapel room in the Shook house until Jacob Shook's death.

Sometime afterward this organized church became known as Louisa Chapel, named after Louisa, daughter of David Parker Jr. and great-granddaughter of Jacob. The name *Louisa* is pronounced as *Lou-'eye-sa*.

I don't think that Jacob could ever visualize that his heirs would someday be counted in the tens of thousands. Neither could he imagine that his descendants would come and worship in this place so dear to his heart, or that we would hold his Chapel Room with such reverence and that we too would feel the Holy Spirit there.

SUNDOWN FOR JACOB AND ISABELLA

Eleven children—six sons and five daughters—were born and lived into adulthood. We *believe* Jacob Jr. was the first born about 1776, followed by John about 1778, Abraham about 1780, Susannah about 1784, Elizabeth about 1785, David in 1786, Peter in 1790, Margaret in 1794, Mary Ann "Polly" in 1796, Catherine in 1798, and Daniel in 1800.

Jacob and Isabella lived a long life together with their large family and all the friends they had met in this valley. They had lived in excess of forty years in the large home that they built on the banks of the Pigeon Their children were now all grown with families of their own. Grandchildren had warmed their hearts, sat on their laps, learned the Bible stories that both loved to tell. Having grandchildren was truly one of God's greatest blessings.

However, their bones hurt, their steps had slowed, their paths not quite as straight, their eyes were dim, and their hearing was not so sharp anymore. Tiredness claimed their bodies. A weariness still hung to them as they arose from their beds each morning was always present.

He had long ago made final arrangements for his next life when he accepted Jesus Christ, the Son of the living God, as his Savior. Isabella had given her life to God long ago. Together they had raised their children, every one of them, in the paths they should go, and their souls were also locked in God's hands. They had fought a good fight and had stayed on the path wherever the Holy Spirit led. Jacob knew it was time to make his final plans on earth.

On July 2, 1836, Jacob wrote his last will and testament. Isabella, his beloved wife, was still living on this date, and he made provisions for her to continue to live in their home with the profits of his plantation for her use for the rest of her life.

THE LAST WILL AND TESTAMENT OF JACOB SHOOK

State of North Carolina—Haywood County

July the second day 1836, in the name of God Amen. I Jacob Shook of the same State and County aforesaid being old but of sound mind and memory and taking into consideration that all men have to die do make this my last Will and Testament. In the first place my will to give my soul to Christ who redeemed it, also my body to be buried in a Christian orderly manner. In the second place that all my honest debts be paid out of my Estate. In the third place it is my will that my beloved wife Isabella have the full possession of my house and plantation during of her natural life and also she be maintained and supported out of the rent of the plantation and stock during her natural life at the discretion of my administrators or Executors.

In the next place I give and bequeath to my son John Shook, one dollar. In the next place I give and bequeath to my son Abraham Shook, one dollar. In the next place I give and bequeath to my son Daniel Shook, one dollar, In the next place I give and bequeath to my son David Shook, one dollar, and in the next place I give and bequeath to my son Peter Shook, one dollar. In the next place I give and bequeath unto my daughter Polly Hanes, one dollar. At or after her death to see all my estate real and personal and at a twelve months credit and divided amongst my children. To Wit: Betsey Hide, Jacob Shook, Susannah Goodson, Peggy or Margaret Hicks and Catherine Cooper, and my will also is that Catherine's part of my estate except one dollar to her own use, and the remainder to be divided amongst Catherine's three children, to Susannah the half, Polly and Uriah the balance. My will is also that Susannah, Catherine's oldest daughter, have one cow and calf, one bed and furniture and S. wheel and cards over and above what was mentioned. I certify this to be my last Will and Testament and revoking all others given under my hand and seal in the presence of, the day and year above written.

Jacob Shook, (seal)
Attest: -
Hodge Rabon
Samuel Smith, Jurat

CLOSURE

Jacob passed away on September 1, 1839. We, his children, can only hope that his death was swift and peaceful. One thing we do have assurance of is that heavenly angels were there ministering to him as well as his earthly family and friends. As he entered the shadow of death, he felt no evil there. Jacob lived ninety years, four months, and eleven days.

We know that Isabella had passed on sometime between the date of his will and his own death because his estate immediately went into probate. This is additional proof that the house was not built for Peter. One mystery about her burial remained and was a concern of some of her descendants currently living. Why did she not have a marker on her grave? It was assumed that the space beside Jacob's resting place is hers. Descendants had a stone placed there with our love, honor, and respect for our grandmother of so long ago. Her stone matches his old stone as closely as could be found.

Jacob and Isabella Shook are buried in Pleasant Hill Cemetery in Clyde, North Carolina. His grave has been honored with a plaque from the Daughters of the American Revolution. His family lay all around him on a hill, underneath dogwood trees. How very fitting that the trees are dogwood trees. Even in death, the symbol of the shed blood of Jesus Christ watches over their earthly remains.

Jacob Shook's grave site

Isabella Weitzel Shook's grave site

Jacob's grave is slightly to the right of center. He is resting among their family.

JACOB SHOOK'S ESTATE INVENTORY SALE

The record of Jacob Shook's estate inventory sale can be found in the Haywood County Courthouse in Waynesville, North Carolina. You will see it in *Wills and Inventories* book # 1, on pages 54, 55, and 56. The quality of the copies of these pages is poor and cannot be included in this book. I have chosen instead to give a description of the sale written by Brenda Hudgins. She described what she might have seen and heard as the sale began. There is a summary of the sale following her description.

> The transcribing of the Estate Sale of Jacob Shook has been a labor of love for my ancestors and the heritage they left for us. I could not

have done this without the help of my husband, H.G, who was a farm boy.

In translating all the items up for sale, my mind began to wander, all the way back to the 1800s, with Papa Jacob and Grandma Isabella. I want to share my thoughts with you and my newly found and already much-loved cousins.

I stand in a crowd of rough, sturdy-looking mountain men and a few of their wives today. I see my great-great grandfather David is here with his brother Peter; and off to the side, I see Mary Shook, widow of Jacob's brother John. Everyone is ready for the auctioneer to start. On sale today are treasures that have been used and loved by our grandparents.

The first item up for bid is Papa's plow. A plow that no doubt he fashioned in his blacksmith's shop. I can see him bent over the fire and the anvil with his tools. Sweat is pouring down his face, and his muscles are bulging as he uses his hammer to forge this plow. I see him later, in the fields with this same plow. A weather-beaten, sunburned old man, stooped from many years of hard labor. He is tilling his fields, his plow hooked up to his old mule, getting ready to sow and plant crops that will ensure that his family can survive another year in this mountain wilderness. "Going, going, gone!" the auctioneer cries. Sold for $1.00. The old mule will be sold too. Papa doesn't need them anymore. His hands have been stilled by death.

The cows are on the block, and they too have been sold. All of Papa's sheep are going too. I look at the sheep, and I can see Papa in the shearing shed, bent over with shears that he made by hand, carefully snipping wool that he will then carry to the house in big baskets. Grandma Isabella and the girls will get to work, washing and cleaning, carding and spinning the wool to make the family clothing for another year.

I watch as the flax wheel and stylards are sold. The churn that she used to make butter, sitting for hours churning for her family, is now another woman's churn.

Oh no! Here comes Papa's coffee mill and his 'shugar' can. Can this be real? I can see Papa and Grandma sitting down after supper to have a cup of coffee together and going over events of their day, smiling at some of the things that have happened today.

Now the auctioneer is selling Grandma's dishes. Her pots and pans and spiders that were made for her by Papa's hands. They were made with love for her to cook their meals over the open fireplace.

They are gone. Someone has bought them. Grandma doesn't need them anymore. Her hands have been stilled by death.

Oats and wheat, barrels that Papa made to carry things from the field, gone. Candle molds, iron foundry tools. Grandma's smoothing iron, all going to someone new. Tool made by this sturdy German farmer to provide for his family are gone from his family forever.

Uncle Peter and Grandpa David are here today, and they are buying some of the things that they used while growing up. What sweet memories they must bring. Mary Shook just bought Grandma's spider. I hope she takes care of it. Grandpa David is buying baskets, barrels, and wool. And look, he is buying Papa's clock! I wonder, did Papa's grandparents bring this clock from Germany? Uncle Peter is buying chairs and tools and sundry articles.

Here comes Papa's tomahawk up next. I wonder, did he make this in his shop? This was one of Papa's most treasured items. I rather think that it was given to him by his Cherokee friends in a great ceremony. Allen Haynes has just bought it for .43 3/4 cents.

Now the auctioneer is holding up Papa's Bible. That precious Bible that guided Papa through hard times and good is being sold. I can see the family gathered around the fire at night, candles giving off just enough light to read by. Papa is reading from God's word, instilling into his children the values to last a lifetime. Papa's face is all alight from the joy that this Book has given him. My heart cries out for one of his children to buy it! Oh, John Snider bought it and Papa's sermon books. John is married to one of Papa's granddaughters, so the book is not lost to all the family. Thank God for this.

Everything is gone now, to new owners who will use them to provide for their families. Everything that was used to make this old house a home is gone now. Gone because Papa Jacob and Grandma Isabella don't need them anymore. Their earthly toils have ended, and they now rest in the arms of Jesus.

I come back to the present, and I believe that Papa and Grandma are smiling down at us. Their family is being reunited once again, and we have their blessings in what we are trying to do. So, cousins, let's go forth and finish what our Papa started!

The Summary of His Estate

The total amount produced by the auction sale of farm equipment, stock and personal property in the estate was $1230.81.

A list of notes owing the estate before the sale listed on the 28th January 1840 (to wit)

One note on Jacob Smith & Nathan Gibson. Principal $81.00
Interest on same $10.50
One Judgment on George Cooper. Principal $29.50
Interest on same $13.31 3/4
One Judgment on George Cooper. Principal $47.50
Interest on same $16.54
One note on David Miller, Principal $50.00
Interest on same $8.50
One note on David Miller. Principal $100.00
Interest on same $11.00
One note on Conrad Rhinehart. Principal $5.00
Interest on same .65 cents
One note on Allen Haynes. Principal $5.00
Interest on same .65 cents
Judgment on Jonas Medford $11.75
Doubtful Notes $390.90 3/4
One note on Albert Robbins. Principal $51.50
Interest on same $78.15

One note on Henry Fulbright. Principal	$48.00
Interest on same $64.48	
One note on Jacob Fulbright. Principal	$88.31
Interest on same $95.37	
One note on Jacob Fulbright. Principal	$22.62
Interest on same $30.08	
	$478.11 1/2

Jacob seemed to be his day's version of our current day's ATM machine.

William Welch, the last and highest bidder, purchased the house and 153 acres of land for $1,200.

CHILDREN AND GRANDCHILDREN OF JACOB AND ISABELLA

(Johann "Jacob"[3] Shook, Johann "George"[2] Schuck, Johannes "John"[1] Schuck) was born 07 April 1749 in Northampton County, Pennsylvania, and died 01 September 1839 in Haywood County, North Carolina. He married Isabella Weitzel around 1775 in North Carolina. She was born around 1755 in Pennsylvania and died before 1839 in Haywood County, North Carolina.

Jacob and Isabella raised eleven children to adulthood. They were the following:

1. (Jacob[4] Shook, Johann "Jacob"[3] Shook, Johann "George"[2] Schuck, Johannes "John"[1] Schuck) Jacob was born around 1776 in Burke County, North Carolina, and died 1858 in Columbia County, Arkansas. He had married Elizabeth, last name unknown.

2. (Elizabeth "Betsy"[4] Shook, Johann "Jacob,"[3] Shook, Johann "George"[2] Schuck, Johannes "John"[1] Schuck) Elizabeth was born on 24 July 1774, Lincoln County North Carolina, and married John Hyde in North Carolina. She died 19 February 1847 in Missouri. No further information was found for her.

The children of Jacob Shook and Elizabeth were the following:

- ❏ John Shook was born around 1806 in Missouri Territory and died before 1860 in Arkansas.
- ❏ Hiram Shook was born around 1809 in Missouri Territory.
- ❏ Mahala Emily Shook was born 25 December 1810 in Missouri Territory and died 21 February 1884 in Arkansas.
- ❏ Daniel Shook was born between 1812 and 1814 in Missouri Territory and died around 1860 in Texas.
- ❏ Nathan Shook was born between 1816 and 1820 in Missouri Territory and died in 1849 in Texas.
- ❏ Elizabeth Shook was between 1816 and 1820 in Missouri Territory.
- ❏ Jefferson Shook was born in 1820 in Madison County, Missouri Territory, and died before 1880 in Cherokee County, Texas.
- ❏ Jacob Wright Shook was born 29 January 1823 in Madison County, Missouri Territory and died in March 1882, in Florida.

Jacob and Elizabeth migrated to the Missouri Territory circa 1827 and began buying land, eventually owning about six hundred acres in what became Ozan, Hemstead County,

Arkansas. Some of his children later migrated on to Texas. There are many of Jacob and Elizabeth's descendants living in Texas now.

3. (John[4] Shook, Johann "Jacob,"[3] Shook, Johann "George"[2] Schuck, Johannes "John"[1] Schuck) was born about 1778 in Burke County, North Carolina. He married Polly Deal. The date of death is unknown. No further information has been found on John. Polly Deal Shook was found in North Carolina. I believe she may have a son who served in the Civil War, but he is not positivity identified.

4. (Abraham[4] Shook, Johan "Jacob"[3] Shook, Johann "George"[2] Schuck, Johannes "John"[1] Schuck) was born about 1783 in Burke County, North Carolina, and died 10 December 1814 in the War of 1812 while serving in Bedford Tennessee. Abraham married Elizabeth C. Buford about 1806 in North Carolina. She was born about 1785 in North Carolina and died after 1815 in North Carolina.

The children of Abraham Shook and Elizabeth Buford Shook were the following:

- ❑ William Buford Shook, born on March 11, 1808, in North Carolina. He died September 16, 1870, in Webster County, Missouri.
- ❑ Rebecca Shook was born in 1810
- ❑ Lucinda Shook was born in 1812

❑ Lurana Shook was born in 1814.

There are many descended from this family who still live in Missouri and in Texas.

5. (Susanna[4] Shook, Johan "Jacob"[3] Shook, Shook, Johann "George"[2] Schuck, Johannes "John"[1] Schuck) was born about 1784 in Burke County, North Carolina. She married Ephraim Goodwin. The date of death is unknown.

The children of Susanna Shook and Ephraim Goodwin were the following:

❑ Ester Goodwin was born about 1813 in South Carolina. She married A. B. Norris, 30 October 1834, Habersham County, Georgia.

❑ Jacob Goodwin was born in 1810, Haywood County, North Carolina. He died in 1865 in Izard County, Arkansas.

❑ Mary D. Goodwin was born around 1814 in Missouri.

I have been unable to find Ephraim and Susannah in the census. My oversight, I'm sure.

I did find Ester and A. B. Norris in Georgia with one son under the age of five years.

6. (David[4] Shook, Johann "Jacob"[3] Shook, Johann "George"[2] Schuck, Johannes "John"[1] Schuck) was born 19 September 1786 in Burke County, North Carolina, and died 21 July 1882 in Haywood County, North Carolina. He married

Sarah Haynes 12 January 1809 in Haywood County, North Carolina.

The children of David and Sarah were the following:

- Elizabeth Ann "Betsey"[5] Shook, born on 06 January 1810 in Haywood County, North Carolina; died 10 December 1872 in North Carolina.
- Mary Louisa "Polly" Shook, born around 1812 in Haywood County, North Carolina; died 14 July 1880. She married George Lewis Cunningham on 10 February 1856, in Haywood County, North Carolina.
- Nancy Janice Shook, born on 07 July 1813 in Haywood County, North Carolina; died on 11 January 1892 in Haywood County, North Carolina.
- Sarah Shook, born on 27 February 1815, Haywood County, North Carolina; died on 14 November 1883 in Haywood County, North Carolina.
- James Mills Shook, born on 10 October 1816 in Haywood County, North Carolina; died on 01 July 1891 in Haywood County, North Carolina.
- Jonathan Shook, born on around 1817 in Haywood County, North Carolina.
- Keziah Caroline Shook, born on around 1818 in Haywood County, North Carolina.

- Ephraim Wesley Shook, born on around 1821, Haywood County, North Carolina; died 12 April 1858 in Haywood County, North Carolina.
- David Parker Shook, born on 03 August 1822 in Haywood County, North Carolina; died 12 August 1902, Haywood County, North Carolina.
- Martha Ann Shook, born on around 1824 in Haywood County, North Carolina; died around 1862 in Haywood County, North Carolina.
- Barbara Shook, born on around 1826 in Haywood County, North Carolina.
- William Lafayette Shook, born on 15 May 1829 in Haywood County, North Carolina; died 17 July 1914 in Buncombe County, North Carolina.
- Telitha Emily Shook, born on March 1830 in Haywood County, North Carolina; died in 1911, Haywood County, North Carolina.
- Jacob D. Shook, born on around 1831 in Haywood County, North Carolina; died 1890 in Haywood County, North Carolina.
- Rufus Mills Shook, born on about 1834 in Haywood County, North Carolina; died 12 November 1861.

David lived beside the Pigeon River all his life. He was a farmer and a leader in the

Methodist church. He assumed responsibilities for the church's work when Jacob became too feeble. This included acting as host for the Shook Campground Meetings. He took an active part, calling the crowds to services with his horn for fifty-one consecutive years. He lived to be ninety-six years old.

Most of David and Sarah's children lived out their lives in western North Carolina. Many are buried in the Pleasant Hill Cemetery in Clyde, North Carolina, along with David and Sarah. Sarah's tombstone is inscribed "Consort of David Shook." We must remember that they lived in the same period as England's Queen Victoria. Queen Victoria called her husband, Prince Albert, her consort. The later generations of their descendants are to be found in all sections of our nation.

7. (Peter[4] Shook, Johann "Jacob"[3] Shook, Johann "George"[2] Schuck, Johannes "John"[1] Schuck) was born on 29 October 1790 in Burke County, North Carolina, and died on 25 December 1855 in Haywood County, North Carolina. His first marriage was to an unknown woman. He married Mahala Evens, daughter of Jacob Evens and Aliff Cooper, around 1814 in Haywood County, North Carolina She was born 11 April 1800 in Buncombe County, North Carolina, and died 06 March 1894 in Haywood County, North Carolina.

Child of Peter Shook and Unknown woman is here.

❑ John[5] Shook, born on around 1812 in Haywood County, North Carolina; died on 08 January 1889, Rabun County, Georgia.

Children of Peter Shook and Mahala Evans Shook were the following:

❑ Levicey Avaline Shook, born on 15 May 1815 in Haywood County, North Carolina; died 19 June 1874, Jackson County, North Carolina.
❑ William Taylor Shook, born on 16 October 1816 in Haywood County, North Carolina; died on 27 June 1889, Haywood County, North Carolina.
❑ Cecila Caroline Shook, born on 09 June 1818 in Haywood County, North Carolina; died 18 July 1898 in Haywood County, North Carolina.
❑ Susan Elmina Shook, born on 13 March 1822 in Haywood County, North Carolina; died 02 February 1892 in Haywood County, North Carolina.
❑ Amanda Shook, born on around 1824 in Haywood County, North Carolina; died in 1845. She married William Grimes.
❑ Julia Elizabeth Shook, born on 13 March 1827, Haywood County, North Carolina;

died 11 July 1913 in Cocke County, Tennessee.
- ❑ Margaret Shook, born on around 1829 in Haywood County, North Carolina.
- ❑ Nancy Adeline Shook, born on 16 July 1832, Haywood County, North Carolina; died 24 April 1878 in Haywood County, North Carolina.
- ❑ Daniel Haskew Shook, born on 16 March 1835, Haywood County, North Carolina; died 12 March 1920 in Buncombe County, North Carolina.

Peter purchased the first home place that Jacob built for his family. This deed is found in the Haywood County Courthouse Book of Deeds, page 384. Jacob sold the house on six acres of land for twelve dollars. The house was known by the residents of Clyde as Mahala's House. She continued to live there until her death at age ninety-four. She lived twenty-nine years as a widow. Two of their daughters, Cecila and Susan, never married and continued to live with their mother.

Peter made many land transactions during his lifetime, as did David. These are all available in the Haywood County, North Carolina, courthouse. Look for the earliest grantee and grantor books.

Peter and Mahala were buried in the Pleasant Hill Cemetery in Clyde, North Carolina. Many of his children and grandchildren were also buried there. The later generations of their descendants scattered into all portions of our nation.

8. (Margaret "Peggy"[4] Shook, Johann "Jacob"[3] Shook, Johann "George"[2] Schuck, Johannes "John"[1] Schuck) was born 04 June 1794 in Buncombe County, North Carolina, and died after 1870 in Greene County, Arkansas. She married Joseph Hicks, son of Jonathan Hicks and Nancy Horne, on 20 November 1817 in Haywood County, North Carolina.

Children of Margaret Hicks and Joseph Hicks were the following:

- ❑ Nancy Isabella Hicks, born on 04 November 1818 in Haywood County, North Carolina; married Asaph H. Battle.
- ❑ Jacob Hicks, born on 13 November 1820 in Haywood County, North Carolina; died on 23 March 1893 in Logan County, Arkansas.
- ❑ Jonathan Hicks, born on 20 January 1823 in Haywood County, North Carolina; died while serving in the War with Mexico.
- ❑ Mahala Hicks, born on 18 August 1825, Haywood Country, North Carolina; married Jarrell Dacus.
- ❑ Elizabeth Elvira Hicks, born on 02 May 1828 in North Carolina; died in Arkansas.

- ❑ Joseph Calloway Hicks, born on 24 March 1830 in Haywood County, North Carolina; died 1877, Craighead County, Arkansas.
- ❑ Margaret Mercillia Hicks, born on 06 August 1822 in Haywood County, North Carolina; married Robert C. Dacus.

Margaret Shook Hicks, widowed, took her family to northeastern Arkansas into Greene County, now Craighead County, and established the Hicks homestead there. She had inherited the land warrant when her unmarried son, Jonathan, was killed in the War with Mexico. Most of their descendants are still in Arkansas. However, many can be found in several other southern states and in California and Washington.

9. (Mary Ann "Polly"[4] Shook, Johann "Jacob"[3] Shook, Johann "George"[2] Schuck, Johannes "John"[1] Schuck) was born 18 January 1796 in Buncombe County, North Carolina. She married John Haynes August 1814 in Haywood County, North Carolina. Details of her death are unknown.

Children of Mary Ann Shook and John Haynes were the following:

- ❑ Isabella R. Haynes, born on 11 September 1815, Haywood County, North Carolina; died 11 December 1895, Haywood County, North Carolina.

- Melinda Haynes, born on 06 February 1817, Missouri.
- Judson Posey Haynes, born on 17 April 1819, Missouri; died 07 January 1877, Haywood County, North Carolina.
- Jacob Shook Haynes, born on 21 January 1821, Missouri.
- Mary "Polly" Haynes, born on 20 December 1822, Missouri.
- David Haynes, born on 25 June 1825, Missouri; died February 1901, Klamath County, Oregon.
- Susanna Haynes, born on June 1827, Haywood County, North Carolina.

The Polly Shook/John Haynes family traveled often. The birth places of their children tell us this. John Haynes was a Baptist minister, and in my mind's eye, I can see this family as they migrate to Missouri. Being somewhat familiar with this state, I can see what their life was about each day. John most likely moved around Missouri every few years, or more often, as he worked with the Baptist Church establishing young churches. He may have worked as the Circuit Riders Ministers did; leaving his family in one established location while he traveled did the church's work for a few weeks before returning home again. He most likely did some farming, growing the food for his animals and family. It was a hard life, but a satisfying one. He brought the family full circle as we see that his youngest child was born in Haywood County, North Carolina, same as his oldest child. John was living in Georgia when he passed away.

10. (Cathrine[4] Shook, Johann "Jacob"[3] Shook, Johann "George"[2] Schuck, Johann "John"[1] Schuck) was born around 1798 in North Carolina and died in Jackson County, North Carolina. She married George Cooper 26 March 1821 in Haywood County, North Carolina.

Child of Catherine Shook and unknown father is.

❑ Susanna Shook, born on October 1819 in Haywood County, North Carolina; died 02 February 1902, Haywood County, North Carolina.

This grandchild has always fascinated me. Was she born out of wedlock? We find no record for an earlier marriage for Catherine. Did Catherine continue to live with her parents for the two years before she married George Cooper? Was Susannah a baby in the Jacob Shook's household? It is apparent from Jacob's will that he favored this granddaughter. Did she spend much time in her papa's lap, pulling on his beard? Susannah was about seven years old when her first half sibling came. I can see her playing with Mary Elmira, also called Polly.

Children of Catherine Shook and George Cooper were the following:

- Mary Elmira "Polly" Cooper, born on 11 March 1822 in Haywood County, North Carolina; died after 1880 in Swain County, North Carolina.
- Uriah Cooper, born on around 1826 in Haywood County, North Carolina; died before 1900 in Swain County, North Carolina.
- Mcanally Cooper, born on around 1838 in Haywood County, North Carolina; died 08 September 1863 in Limestone, Washington County, Tennessee.
- Green Berry Cooper, born on 23 August 1844 in Cherokee County, North Carolina; died 07 Sep 1914, Haywood County, North Carolina.

Catherine and George lived out their lives in North Carolina. It is unknown where their children were.

11. (Daniel[4] Shook, Johann "Jacob"[3] Shook, Johann "George"[2] Schuck, Johannes "John"[1] Schuck) was born around 1800 in Haywood County, North Carolina.

There is no existing further information regarding Daniel.

JACOB'S DESCENDANTS IN THE CIVIL WAR

Throughout this book, the main focus has been on Jacob. The Civil War period began some twenty years after his demise. His descendants who fought in this war are best identified as being children of his children. This is especially important when there are cousins with the same name belonging to different parents. In this chapter Civil War veterans will be listed under their parent's name. All eleven of Jacob's children will be listed here, whether or not they had a veteran son. None will be omitted and left in doubt.

1. (Jacob,[4] Johann "Jacob,"[3] Shook, Johann "George"[2] Schuck, Johannes "John"[1] Schuck) Jacob married Elizabeth, last name unknown No record has been discovered on any children being a Civil War veteran in this family.

2. (John,[5] Jacob,[4] Johann "Jacob,"[3] Shook, Johann "George"[2] Schuck, Johannes "John"[1] Schuck) John married Polly Deal. Their son was:

    ❑ William Shook, Confederate side, Eighth Arkansas Infantry, Company B, ranked in and out as a private.

3. (William Buford[5] Shook, Abraham[4] Shook, Johann "Jacob,"[3] Shook, Johann "George"[2]

Schuck, Johannes "John"[1] Schuck) William Buford Shook married Mary Elizabeth Acuff. Their sons were the following:

- Joseph B. Shook, Union, Sixteenth Regiment, Missouri Cavalry, Company D, private.
- William Lafayette Shook, Union, First Regiment, Missouri Cavalry, Company H, private.

William Lafayette Shook of MO and TX

- Jacob Shook, Union, Sixteenth Regiment, Missouri Cavalry, Company D, private.

Note: Joseph and Jacob served in the same regiment and company at the same time. Many of the Shook family members did this. Joseph and Jacob were Jacob's great-grandsons.

4. (Susannah[4] Shook, Johann Johann "Jacob,"[3] Shook, Johann "George"[2] Schuck, Johannes "John"[1] Schuck) Susanna Shook married Ephraim Goodwin. No record has been discovered on any children being a Civil War veteran in this family.
5. (Elizabeth Ann "Betsy"[5] Shook, David,[4] Shook, Johann "Jacob"[3] Shook, Johann "George"[2] Schuck, Johannes "John"[1] Schuck) Elizabeth "Betsey" Shook married Joshua Kinsland. Their sons were the following:

- ❏ William M Kinsland, Confederate side, Sixty-Second Regiment, North Carolina Infantry, Company C, private
- ❏ Jesse E. Kinsland, Confederate, Sixty-Second Regiment, North Carolina Infantry, Company C, private.

  Note: These two brothers served in the same regiment and company.

6. (David[4] Shook, Johann "Jacob,"[3] Shook, Johann "George"[2] Schuck, Johannes "John"[1] Schuck) David married Sarah Haynes. Their sons were the following:

- ❏ William Lafayette Shook, Confederate side, Sixty-Second North Carolina Infantry, Company C. Enlisted as a private on July 11, 1862, and mustered out as a sergeant on May 10, 1865. William L. was with the Sixty-Second Regiment in December 1862 at Zollicoffer Station, Tennessee. He was a prisoner of war.

William Lafayette Shook and wife Sarah of Buncombe County, North Carolina.

- Jacob D. Shook, Confederate side, Fifty-Eighth North Carolina Infantry, Company D. Enlisted as a private on June 27, 1863, age seventeen. Jacob D. *did not survive this war*. He died on December 31, 1863, at Dalton, Georgia.
- Rufus Mills Shook, Confederate side, Twenty-Fifth Regiment, North Carolina Infantry, Company C. Private. *Rufus did not survive this war.* He died November 12, 1861, in Camp Davis, North Carolina.

Sarah[5] Shook, (David[4] Shook, Johann "Jacob"[3] Shook, Johann "George"[2] Schuck, Johannes "John"[1] Schuck), Sarah married Peter Synder (Snider).

Sarah and Peter's sons were the following:

- ❏ John W. Synder (Snider) was Jacob Shook's great-grandson. Notes for John W. Snider: Confederate, Sixty-Second Regiment, North Carolina Infantry, Company C. John W. enlisted as a private in Buncombe County on 24 October 1861 and mustered out on 15 April 1862.
- ❏ Jonathan M. Synder (Snider) Confederate, Forty-Fourth Regiment, North Carolina Infantry, Company K, private.

The portrait hanging over the mantel in the living room of the Shook Museum is of Sarah and Peter Snider. She is Jacob and Isabella's granddaughter. This is the family that purchased Jacob's Bible at his estate inventory sale.

(Nancy[5] Shook, David[4] Shook, Johann "Jacob"[3] Shook, Johann "George"[2] Schuck, Johannes "John"[1] Schuck) Nancy Shook married Thomas L. Snyder. Their son was:

- ❏ Thomas L. Snyder (Snider) was Jacob Shook's great-grandson. Confederate, Twenty-Fifth Regiment, North Carolina Infantry, Company C. Rank in as private;

mustered out as sergeant. He lost his left foot in battle.

(Samantha Josephine[6] Clark, Martha Ann[5] Shook, David[4] Shook, Johann "Jacob"[3] Shook, Johann "George"[2] Schuck, Johannes "John"[1] Schuck) Samantha married Francis M. Snider.

- ❑ Francis M. Snider, (Samantha's husband) was Jacob's great-grandson-in-law. Confederate side, Twenty-Fifth Regiment, North Carolina Infantry, Company C, private.

David had three sons, three grandsons, and one grandson-in-law to serve in the Civil War. Two sons, John D. and Rufus Mills, did not survive.

7. (Peter[5] Shook, Johann "Jacob"[3] Shook, Johann "George"[2] Schuck, Johannes "John"[1] Schuck) Peter married Mahala Evans. Their sons were the following:

- ❑ William T. Shook, Confederate, Eighth Battalion, North Carolina Junior Reserves, Company B, private
- ❑ Daniel Haskew Shook, Confederate side, Sixty-Second Regiment, North Carolina Infantry, Company C, private.

(John[5] Shook, Peter[4] Shook, Johann "Jacob,"[3] Shook, Johann "George"[2] Schuck, Johann

GREATER THAN THE MOUNTAINS WAS HE   159

"John"[1] Schuck) John married Jane Nicholson. Their sons were the following:

- W. Lafayette Shook, Confederate, Fifty-Second Regiment, Georgia Infantry, Company F, private. He *did not survive this war* and died 17 June 1862. This W. Lafayette Shook was Jacob and Isabella's great-grandson.

(John Hawkins[6] Shook, John[5] Shook, Peter[4] Shook, Johann "Jacob"[3] Shook, Johann "George"[2] Schuck, Johannes "John"[1] Schuck)

- John Hawkins Shook, Confederate side, Fifty-Second Regiment, Georgia Infantry, Company F, private. John was marked for distinguished service. John Hawkins Shook was Jacob and Isabella's great-grandson.

John Hawkins Shook

(Alexander S.[6] Shook, John[5] Shook, Peter[4] Shook, Johann "Jacob"[3] Shook, Johann "George"[2] Schuck, Johannes "John"[1] Schuck) This Alexander S. Shook was Jacob and Isabella's great-grandson.

❑ Alexander S.[6] Shook, Confederacy, Fifty-Second Regiment, Georgia Infantry, Company E, private. Enlisted March 4, 1862. Severely wounded on July 22, 1864, and furloughed at home in Towns County, Georgia, through the close of war. He was born 05 May 1840 in Union County, Georgia. He married Tennessee Cantrell.

8. (Margaret "Peggy"[4] Shook, Johann "Jacob"[3] Shook, Johann "George"[2] Schuck, Johannes "John"[1] Schuck) Margaret Shook married Joseph Hicks. Their son was Joseph Calloway Hicks

❑ Joseph Calloway Hicks, Confederate side, Thirtieth Regiment Arkansas Infantry, Companies H and K, private. Joseph Calloway was born 24 March 1830 in Haywood County, North Carolina, and died in 1877 in Craighead County, Arkansas. He married Margaret C. Davis. Joseph Calloway Hicks is this author's great-grandfather.

Joseph Calloway Hicks

JOSEPH CALLOWAY HICKS'S CIVIL WAR LETTER TO HIS WIFE, COPIED EXACTLY AS WRITTEN.

Camp Bayou Meter

September the 25th, 1862

My dear and well beloved Margarett and children.

    I have an opportunity of sending you a few lines and I thought I would do so to let you no {know} that I was still well. I have nothing much to wright. I want to see you and the children very bad. Margarett my sweet child – I dream of you every night. I dreampt last night of having you in my arms. I wish to god it could be so. I can't tell when I will have a chance of coming home for the officers here are very tite. They won't give any furlows at all. If I think there is any possible chance for one the last of next month or the first of the month after I intend to try to get it and come home and gather the corn but if I don't come try to have it gathered the first of November. We have orders to be ready to leave here next Tuesday morning and go to Springfield Missouri. Margarett I want you to do the best you can for yourself and the children. Mr. Newsom came in here today and told me there was salt (?) to sell at Old Town on the Mississippi River. I hope James Kitchens has got some for you. If he has not try to get him to get some for you as much as possible. Tell him to get the worth of that ten dollar bill I left and try to get a side of upper leather and a side of sole leather from Mr. Baker. If he won't let _____ (bottom of Page 1 cut off).

(top of Page 2)

Margarett my dear god love you I wish I could be with you _____ tell our children that I love them but if I never get home any more raise them as they should be raised. Excuse my bad writing for I have sliped off down in to a creek bottom and am writing on my nea {knee} no more at present but remaining yours until death.

J C Hicks
To Margarett Hicks

I want you to phrase your own letters and I wish you could write your own.

So fare well sweet
Margarett

Note: The following is written upside down as if the letter were folded, and this is the address on the outside:

Margarett C Hicks
Greenboro Ark.

9. (Mary Ann "Polly"[4] Shook, Johann "Jacob,"[3] Shook, Johann "George"[2] Schuck, Johannes

"John"[1] Schuck) Mary Ann Shook married John Haynes. Their sons were the following:

- Judson P. Haynes, Confederate side, Twenty-Ninth North Carolina Infantry, Company E, private.
- David Haynes, Confederate side, Fifth Regiment, North Carolina Senior Reserve, Company K, private
- Jacob Shook Haynes. This son probably belongs here; however, there are a number of Jacob Haynes serving on Confederate side from North Carolina. I could not, in good faith, determine their parentage. Many times, the middle name or initial were not included on all records.

10. (Catherine[4] Shook, Johann "Jacob,"[3] Shook, Johann "George"[2] Schuck, Johannes "John"[1] Schuck) Catherine Shook married George Cooper. Their sons were the following:

- Uriah Cooper, Confederate side, Second Regiment, North Carolina Junior Reserve, Company A, private.
- McAnnally Cooper, Confederate side, Second Regiment North Carolina Junior Reserve, Thomas Legion, Company H, private C. McAnnally *did not survive this war*. He died on 08 September 1863, Limestone, Washington County, Tennessee.

- ❏ Green Berry Cooper, Confederate side, Second Regiment North Carolina Cavalry, Nineteen State Troops, Company A, private.

    (What parent would name a son Green Berry? Think of all the teasing he must have endured as he was growing up.)

11. (Daniel[4] Shook, Shook, Johann "Jacob,"[3] Shook, Johann "George"[2] Schuck, Johannes "John"[1] Schuck) Daniel Shook married Emily, unknown last name. There were no Civil War veterans found for Daniel's family.

Twenty-five Civil War veterans have been located and their parentage verified as being among the descendants of Jacob Shook and Isabella Weitzel Shook. There may be others not identified at this time. There are many more Shooks who were Civil War veterans. They are descended from other sons of George Shook and Elizabeth Grub Shook. These were Jacob's nephews who are from Catawba and other Counties.

The Shook veterans are an honored group of strong men. Some served honorably on both sides in this war.

In every case, a great sacrifice was made by the veteran and by their families left behind. Some paid the ultimate price with their lives. Others were horribly wounded and carried those scars through their lives.

To all of them, we owe respect and gratitude. These men and their families picked up their lives and carried on in the tradition set for them by their ancestor, Johann Jacob Shook.

THE HOUSE AS JACOB BUILT IT

Picture of the Shook house as seen in 2003.

JACOB'S CONSTRUCTION

Jacob built four rooms over four rooms, with a full attic on the third floor that he built to be used for worship.

He built a turned stairs in the center of the house where the corner of these four room met. The shadows of these stair risers are plainly seen today and are protected by a sheet of Plexiglass.

In the roof structure just to the north of the center of the house, a small portion of a chimney is visible from the front yard. This marks the width of the original structure. The original structure and the later additional structure are clearly identified in the framing of the attic. The extension of the original attic framing over the present porch also confirms the existence of an original porch.

The square southeast rooms on the first and second floors are the largest of earliest surviving rooms. It is evident that there were rooms where the present-day halls are on the first and second floors and narrow rooms behind the large rooms. So we have a picture of two larger rooms, one on each floor, with smaller rooms around them. These smaller rooms were probably sleeping rooms.

The one massive chimney served large fireplaces in both of the large rooms. Looking closely at the foundation of this chimney, we see that a more modern structure sits on several courses of sun-dried brick, set on large flat stones. This chimney appears to have been rebuilt as early as the mid-nineteenth century.

There is no evidence that cooking was ever done in either fireplace. It was traditional in that period to build a kitchen separated from the main house as a precaution against fire.

There is so much to say about the house. Significant physical evidence from the house's early period survives in the two large southeast rooms. A million words cannot describe it. In my attempt to do so, I want to use parts of a report done in 1995 by A. L. Honeycutt Jr. and John Horton in the Restoration Services Branch of the North Carolina State Historic Preservation Office.

This preliminary reading for the Shook-Smathers house was prepared for the then current and local house preservation committee. Mr. Honeycutt and Mr. Horton have this to say about this physical evidence.

> The door leading from the hall to the first floor parlor is a fine six-paneled door of Georgian-style. Three panels on the door are raised on both sides which is an unusual feature for the western part of the state. There are ghost marks along the top and bottom rails of the door that indicate the door was originally hung with wrought iron strap hinges. The present hinges appear to be late nineteenth-century cast iron butts. There is evidence of extreme weathering on one side of the door, suggesting that it may have originally been an exterior door relocated to this location during the late nineteenth-century renovations.
>
> The door to the second floor southeast room is similar to the first floor parlor door except that there is not evidence for an earlier strap hinge. Instead the door is hung with cast iron butt hinges which appear to be contemporary with the door. The hinges are a fast-joint, three-knuckle type, 2-1/4 inches wide by 3 inches long. The word "Patent" is stamped into one of the leaves. The screws for these hinges are flat tipped instead of gimlet pointed. This evidence suggest that they were in place prior to 1846. The lockset is a mid to late-nineteenth century cast iron rim-lock. Leading to the attic stair, a six-panel door of similar raised panels style exhibits the same type of "Patent" butt hinges.

The first floor parlor door casing is late-nineteenth-century in character. However, this trim has been installed over earlier casing that exhibits a beaded edge. This earlier trim was apparently set flush with the sheathing in the room.

The fireplace surround in the first floor parlor, appears to be a late-nineteenth-century feature with its sawn and turned work and overmantle. The second floor room, the fireplace surround is a very distinctive vernacular Georgian-style paneled wall with arched firebox.

The framing in the attic is of pegged mortise-and-tendon construction, with studs and braces fastened by machine cut nails with handmade heads. The rafters are joined at the ridge with a lapped joint and are pegged. The room is sheathed in wide unfinished boards. The framing lumber in the attic appears to be pit sawn, which is consistent with the circa 1795 construction date. Around the edge of the stair is an exceptionally fine vernacular balustrade. Its construction and detailing are consistent with the other early features in the house. The paneling in the attic stairway is also very well detailed and, together with the quality of the balustrade, suggest that the attic room was intended to be seen as finished space.

In conclusion, there are several early features in these two rooms, much of which supports the circa 1795 construction date.

THE HOUSE AFTER JACOB

William Welch was the best and last bidder for the house and 153 acres of land as part of Jacob's inventory sale. He was an officer in the Haywood County court. His name appears on many documents of all kinds. There is no indication that he ever lived in the house himself. This deed was recorded in Haywood County Courthouse, Book F, page 245. Mr. Welch kept the house for ten years.

Levi Smathers purchased the house from William Welch in 1850. His son, D. I. L. "Dock" Smathers, inherited the house from Levi in 1896. The Smathers family enlarged the house, nearly doubling its size, by adding a stack of four bedrooms, a kitchen, and a utility porch, which was later enclosed to make a utility room. They also added the first- and second-floor porches across the end. Changes were made in rooms that Jacob had built. The wide halls were made on the first and second floors from rooms that were likely used as bedrooms for Jacob's family. The dining room was enlarged and elaborately finished with ceiling beams, wall paneling with a plate rail, and a fireplace. Windows and doors were moved and others added. The chapel room continued to be a place of honor through D. I. L.'s ownership.

Mary Smathers Morgan became the next owner, inheriting the house from her parents. Mary lived in the house until her death in 1981. Her two daughters, Lucille and Ruth, became its next owners. Lucille had passed away, thus passing her share of the house to her son and daughter. Ruth became the person most in charge. However, no one else ever lived in the house. When I first saw the house in 2000, it still held Mary's personal property, and it looked as if Mary had just stepped out. A dress lay across her neatly made bed, and the breakfast table was set as if the family would be called to breakfast at any moment. The twenty years that the house sat empty of family life took a severe toll on the building. The house was in deplorable condition. The 1890s addition was pulling away from the original building. This created a wide crack just under the eaves that could be clearly seen from the attic. This is just one of many things that were wrong. It was obvious that the house would not stand many more years unless repaired immediately.

When I was there in 2001, and with permission to hold an open house, several of the local folks and members of the Smathers family told me about the different times others wanted to purchase the house with a number of possible uses for it in mind. However, Ruth was never satisfied with any of these offers. She wanted the old home restored and used in a way that would be of honorable service while maintaining the integrity and architectural and historical significance of the structure. Dr. Joseph S. Hall, a great-great-great-grandson of Jacob Shook, remembered seeing the house when he was a young boy. He made an offer and had a plan that pleased Ruth in 2003. So he stepped forward and started the process in motion.

Dr. Hall hired the very best restoration to be found in North Carolina. There are not enough words, nor space in this book, to list all that has been accomplished. The work was done under the guidance of the North Carolina Preservation Society. By the end of 2005, the house had been completely renovated and restored. The structure was made solid again. Porches were completely replaced. New posts were duplicated from the pattern of the old post. The porch railings were replaced with wood railings. Layers of wall covering inside the house were removed to show Jacob's original hand-cut wide boards from virgin timber. All work was done with the intent to show the two periods of construction, and a marvelous job was accomplished. The "ghost" of Jacob's stacked stairs in the center of the house was uncovered and is plainly seen. This is now protected by a covering of Plexiglas. The old minister's signature wall between the windows in the chapel room is also protected by Plexiglas. Artifacts found in the house and on the property are now displayed in the house, along with gifted items belonging to generations of Shook and Smathers family members. The chapel room has been kept just as it was in Jacob's time. The generations of Smathers families are to be given credit and appreciation for keeping the old precious room as it was built. The room has been rededicated to God. It is a holy place. Anyone who has the Holy Spirit of God living within their hearts can feel the history of this special place upon entering it. In our mind's eye and ears, we can hear the old hymns being sung, see the old Bibles opened, and hear the scripture read. We can hear the prayers and the sermons, all echoes that make our hearts glad.

In the spring of 2006, the Shook descendants gathered there for a weekend of cousins' reunion. One hundred and twenty of us descendants came from outside the state of North Carolina. The total count, with the local descendants added, was never taken. We toured the old home. We marveled over the beautiful restoration that had been completed. We visited the cemetery and paid our respects to our ancestors there. We attended a Sunday morning service in Louisa Chapel. We tried to express our gratitude to Dr. Hall for his gift. We found that words were not enough, but we did our best. Family histories, stories, and pictures were shared. How proud we were just to be together and to be Shook kids.

The house name is now registered as the Shook Museum, *at* the Shook-Smathers House. There is a website dedicated to it: www.shookmuseum.org. There are several pictures posted here, along with the current information for all activities, including scheduled tours. The house has been placed on the National Registry of Historical Places. The Shook Museum has been selected for the 2011 Best of Clyde Award in the museum category by the US Commerce Association. This award program recognizes outstanding local businesses throughout the country. Each year, the USCA identifies companies that they believe have achieved exceptional success in their local community. We were honored to have received this award.

Dr. Hall gifted the Shook Museum and Shook-Smathers House to the Haywood County Historical Genealogy Society in December of 2011. This society will keep the property maintained, staffed, and open for public tours on a schedule. This place played a great part in God's service during our nation's early years. I believe God still has a use for the old place.

The Shook House as it looks today

Side view of the Shook House as it looks today

The Chapel Room as it looks today

In closing this book I wish to share with you a Smathers's story centering in the chapel room. I found this story on a tattered and aged piece of paper tacked to the wall. This is certainly part of oral history that has been handed down.

THE MISSING BOARD

This missing board used to hold a large number of wooden pegs that the men used to hang up their coats and hats during services in this Upper Room. During the early years of the Smathers' ownership, visitors to this room would ask if they might "have just one peg?" Each one hoping that their peg would have been the one that the Bishop Asbury hung his hat on. Over the years, all of the pegs were given away. Then a visitor asked Mr. Samthers if he could have the board on which they had been. Being a person whom Smathers didn't want to say no to, he was given the whole board. The new owner of the board was a whittler, and he used it all making souvenirs. Mr. Smathers received a knife handle.

The missing board

BIBLIOGRAPHY

Blackmon, Ora. *Western North Carolina: Its Mountains and Peoples to 1880.* Boone, North Carolina: Appalachian Consortium Press, 1977. LCC# 76-53030.

Allen, W.C. The annals of Haywood County, North Carolina, Waynesville, North Carolina, privately published, 1935.

Boehm, Henry. *Reminiscences, Historical and Biographical: Sixty-Four Years in the Ministry.* New York, NY: Carlton and Porter, 1865. From Microfilm WCU Hunter Library, no. 131, roll 9.

Clark, Elmer. Methodism in Western North Carolina, 1966.

Eaker, Lorena Shell. *German-Speaking People West of the Catawba River in North Carolina 1750–1800.* Franklin, North Carolina: Genealogy Publishing Service, 1994. ISBN 1-881851-05-2.

Francis Asbury in North Carolina, with Introductory Notes by Grady L. E. Carroll. Nashville, Tennessee: Parthenon Press, 1977.

Griffin, Clarence. *History of Old Tryon and Rutherford Counties North Carolina 1730–1936.* Spartanburg, South Carolina: reprint by Co Publishers, 1977. ISBN 0-87152-252-7.

King, Duane. *The Cherokee Indian Nation: A Troubled History.* Knoxville, Tennessee: University of Tennessee Press, 1979. ISBN 0-87049-227-6.

Lumpkin, Henry. *From Savannah to Yorktown: The American Revolution in the South.* New York: Paragon

House, 1981. Originally published University of SC Press. ISBN 0 913729-48-5.

McCall, Wm. A. *Cherokees and Pioneers*. Asheville, North Carolina: The Stephens Press, 1952.

Medford, W. Clark. *The Early History of Haywood County*. Asheville, North Carolina: Miller Printing Co., 1961.

Medford, W Clark. *Haywood's Heritage and Finest Hour*. Asheville, North Carolina: Daniels Graphics, 1971.

Medford, W Clark. *Mountain People, Mountain Times*. Asheville, North Carolina: Miller Publishing Co., 1963.

Smith, Mark. *Lifting High the Cross for 200 Years, St. John's Lutheran Church*. Baltimore, Maryland: Gateway Press, 1998. LCC# 98-70604.

Sondley, F. A. *History of Buncombe County North Carolina*. Spartanburg, South Carolina: reprint by Co Publishers, 1977. Reproduced from a 1930 volume, Advocate, Asheville. ISBN 0-87152-253.

Jones, Robert 'Bob', text from www.shookhistory.org family website.